THIRD EDITION

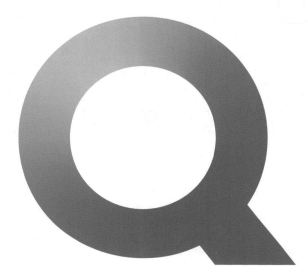

Skills for Success
LISTENING AND SPEAKING

2

Margaret Brooks

OXFORD
UNIVERSITY PRESS

OXFORD
UNIVERSITY PRESS

198 Madison Avenue
New York, NY 10016 USA

Great Clarendon Street, Oxford, OX2 6DP, United Kingdom

Oxford University Press is a department of the University of Oxford.
It furthers the University's objective of excellence in research, scholarship,
and education by publishing worldwide. Oxford is a registered trade
mark of Oxford University Press in the UK and in certain other countries

First published in 2020

2024 2023 2022 2021 2020

10 9 8 7 6 5 4 3 2 1

No unauthorized photocopying

ISBN: 978 0 19 490514 5   STUDENT BOOK 2 WITH IQ ONLINE PACK
ISBN: 978 0 19 490502 2   STUDENT BOOK 2 AS PACK COMPONENT
ISBN: 978 0 19 490538 1   IQ ONLINE STUDENT WEBSITE

Printed in China

This book is printed on paper from certified and well-managed sources

ACKNOWLEDGMENTS

Back cover photograph: Oxford University Press building/David Fisher
Illustration by: p. 26 Karen Minor

*The Publishers would like to thank the following for their kind permission to
reproduce photographs and other copyright material:* **123RF:** pp. 44 (log
house/Benoit Daoust), (Gaudi house/Aliaksandr Mazurkevich), 50 (road
rage/Antonio Diaz), 89 (friends interacting during meal/Mark Bowden),
141 (yurt/Gilad Fiskus), 154 (coastline/bloodua); **Alamy:** pp. 12 (bookshop
café/Luis Dafos), 13 (booksigning/Jeff Morgan 08), 16 (wearing same
shoes/Glasshouse Images), 18 (cyclist in city traffic/Scott Hortop Travel),
28 (cryptic frog/Dave and Sigrun Tollerton), 33 (colourful building/
Maria Galan), 34 (house in Asir/ERIC LAFFORGUE), 37 (white living
room/Jodie Johnson), 38 (red fire truck/imageBROKER), 52 (crowded
bus/Torontonian), 58 (adults talking on balcony/Hero Images Inc.),
62 (Franklin Roosevelt/From Original Negative), (John Kennedy/Trinity
Mirror /Mirrorpix), 76 (interacting with digital assistant/Image navi –
QxQ images), 77 (GPS in car/age fotostock), 79 (1920s miners cottages/
Allan Cash Picture Library), 93 (two sets of identical twins/Image Source
Plus), 94 (male identical twins/Esther Moreno), 98 (multigenerational
family/Kirn Vintage Stock), 116 (adult playing video game/ZUMA Press,
Inc.), 123 (chess trophy/Kirn Vintage Stock), 146 (nomad family/Lucy
Calder), 162 (irrigation sprinklers/Mauritius images GmbH), 165 (children
carrying water/Jake Lyell), 168 (washing hands/Cultura Creative (RF)),
169 (indoor play area/Piotr Adamowicz), 171 (stomachache/Panther Media
GmbH); **Getty:** pp. cover (Green color tile pattern/Fabian Krause/EyeEm),
4 (pet rocks/Al Freni), 5 (foot boats/Keystone/Stringer), 6 (old lightbulb/
Science & Society Picture Library), 9 (organic vegetables/DOUGBERRY),
11 (bookshop/whitemay), 14 (Kente fabric weaving/Education Images),
23 (young women shopping/Peter Cade), 24 (chameleon/Juan Buitrago),
31 (bowerbird/Education Images), 37 (colourful living room/irina88w),
46 (helping elderly woman/SolStock), 48 (work colleagues heated
discussion/praetorianphoto), 56 (attentive student classroom/skynesher),
67 (family meal/Ken Seet/Corbis/VCG), 68 (playing board games/Hero
Images Inc.), 71 (man on laptop/supersizer), 75 (Tanja Hollander/Portland

Press Herald), 83 (woman looking sad/EXTREME-PHOTOGRAPHER), 90
(large family photo/Amrish Saini/EyeEm), 96 (female twins/serts), 105
(looking at photographic memories/Yevgen Timashov), 107 (mother
and daughter with photo album/RapidEye), 111 (grandmother greeting
daughter/Ariel Skelley), 112 (girls playing video game/DaniloAndjus),
117 (father and son playing video game/Tom Werner), 118 (improve
coordination/Jgalione), 120 (children chess tournament/Hero Images),
121 (Students Play Chess/VCG/Contributor), 124 (chess tournament/
VCG), 128 (game developers/AFP), 136 (family playing cricket/uniquely
india), 137 (family playing card game/shapecharge), 138 (cottage in
mountains/Pete Rowbottom), 149 (modern apartment/pawel. gaul), 155
(Bosco Verticale building/marcociannarel), 157 (television interview/vm),
159 (cave dwellings/Alex Lapuerta), 160 (street cleaner/by MedioTuerto),
169 (outdoor play area/Susanne Kronholm), 176 (shipwrecked man/Martin
Barraud), 178 (cattle drinking from stream/Damian Davies), 183 (woman
cleaning house/Tony Hutchings); **Newscom:** p. 34 (Luis Barragán home/
Javier Lira/Notimex); **OUP:** pp. 70 (woman at telegraph/Shutterstock/
Everett Collection), 99 (DNA/Shutterstock /zffoto), 121–122 (chess pieces/
Shutterstock/Nilotic); **Shutterstock:** pp. 2 (queue for Apple store/
Sascha Steinbach/EPA-EFE/Shutterstock), 7 (velocipede/Imfoto), (fidget
spinner/Olga V Kulakova), 19 (frustrated businessman/Creativa Images),
27 (cat/osobystist), 28 (false leaf katydid/PeingjaiChiangmai), (poison
dart frog/Brandon Alms), 30 (monarch butterfly/Kate Scott), (zebras/
The Maberhood), (coral snake/Mark_Kostich), (arctic fox in summer/
COULANGES), (arctic fox in winter/JoannaPerchaluk), 40 (red jacket/
Neamov), (red shoes/Chiyacat), 44 (modern city apartment/Trong Nguyen),
(trailer home/Lowphoto), 51 (radio interview/antoniodiaz), 55 (disruptive
students/Proshkin Aleksandr), 72 (woman using social media/Rawpixel.
com), 86 (man gesturing confused/PicMy), 92 (left family portrait/
Monkey Business Images), (right family portrait/Asia Images Group), 108
(two people talking/yurakrasil), 114 (Monopoly board/enchanted_fairy),
115 (Scrabble/Wachiwit), 118 (reduce stress/Aquarius Studio), (use as a
learning tool/Rawpixel.com), (practice skills/Gorodenkoff), 125 (students
on computers/mofaez), 126 (Simcity game/Pe3k), (phone screen/Stanisic
Vladimir), 127 (adults playing board game/Standret), 130 (adults playing
charades/Syda Productions), 132 (bowling/Corepics VOF), 133 (hide and
seek/Iakov Filimonov), 140 (goats/Travel Pass Photos), 142 (wolf/Alexandr
Kucheryavko), 143 (nomad herding livestock/CW Pix), 147 (high rise
apartments/Naeblys), 149 (woman looking out of window/shurkin_son),
156 (person in Antarctica/Marcelo Alex), 158 (futuristic settlement on
mars/ustas7777777), 164 (dry river bed/Peter Turner Photography),
170 (hand sanitizer/Elizaveta Galitckaia), 171 (cold/aslysun), 180 (water
depth gauges/prajit48), 181 (wall sanitizer/Alexander Oganezov);
Third party: p. 114 (Landlord's game/Thomas E Forsyth).

ACKNOWLEDGMENTS

We would like to acknowledge the teachers from all over the world who participated in the development process and review of *Q: Skills for Success* Third Edition.

USA

Kate Austin, Avila University, MO; **Sydney Bassett**, Auburn Global University, AL; **Michael Beamer**, USC, CA; **Renae Betten**, CBU, CA; **Pepper Boyer**, Auburn Global University, AL; **Marina Broeder**, Mission College, CA; **Thomas Brynmore**, Auburn Global University, AL; **Britta Burton**, Mission College, CA; **Kathleen Castello**, Mission College, CA; **Teresa Cheung**, North Shore Community College, MA; **Shantall Colebrooke**, Auburn Global University, AL; **Kyle Cooper**, Troy University, AL; **Elizabeth Cox**, Auburn Global University, AL; **Ashley Ekers**, Auburn Global University, AL; **Rhonda Farley**, Los Rios Community College, CA; **Marcus Frame**, Troy University, AL; **Lora Glaser**, Mission College, CA; **Hala Hamka**, Henry Ford College, MI; **Shelley A. Harrington**, Henry Ford College, MI; **Barrett J. Heusch**, Troy University, AL; **Beth Hill**, St. Charles Community College, MO; **Patty Jones**, Troy University, AL; **Tom Justice**, North Shore Community College, MA; **Robert Klein**, Troy University, AL; **Patrick Maestas**, Auburn Global University, AL; **Elizabeth Merchant**, Auburn Global University, AL; **Rosemary Miketa**, Henry Ford College, MI; **Myo Myint**, Mission College, CA; **Lance Noe**, Troy University, AL; **Irene Pannatier**, Auburn Global University, AL; **Annie Percy**, Troy University, AL; **Erin Robinson**, Troy University, AL; **Juliane Rosner**, Mission College, CA; **Mary Stevens**, North Shore Community College, MA; **Pamela Stewart**, Henry Ford College, MI; **Karen Tucker**, Georgia Tech, GA; **Loreley Wheeler**, North Shore Community College, MA; **Amanda Wilcox**, Auburn Global University, AL; Heike Williams, Auburn Global University, AL

Canada

Angelika Brunel, Collège Ahuntsic, QC; **David Butler**, English Language Institute, BC; **Paul Edwards**, Kwantlen Polytechnic University, BC; **Cody Hawver**, University of British Columbia, BC; **Olivera Jovovic**, Kwantlen Polytechnic University, BC; **Tami Moffatt**, University of British Columbia, BC; **Dana Pynn**, Vancouver Island University, BC

Latin America

Georgette Barreda, SENATI, Peru; **Claudia Cecilia Díaz Romero**, Colegio América, Mexico; **Jeferson Ferro**, Uninter, Brazil; **Mayda Hernández**, English Center, Mexico; **Jose Ixtaccihusatl**, Instituto Tecnológico de Tecomatlán, Mexico; **Andreas Paulus Pabst**, CBA Idiomas, Brazil; **Amanda Carla Pas**, Instituição de Ensino Santa Izildinha, Brazil; **Allen Quesada Pacheco**, University of Costa Rica, Costa Rica; **Rolando Sánchez**, Escuela Normal de Tecámac, Mexico; **Luis Vasquez**, CESNO, Mexico

Asia

Asami Atsuko, Women's University, Japan; **Rene Bouchard**, Chinzei Keiai Gakuen, Japan; **Francis Brannen**, Sangmyung University, South Korea; **Haeyun Cho**, Sogang University, South Korea; **Daniel Craig**, Sangmyung University, South Korea; **Thomas Cuming**, Royal Melbourne Institute of Technology, Vietnam; **Jissen Joshi Daigaku**, Women's University, Japan; **Nguyen Duc Dat**, OISP, Vietnam; **Wayne Devitte**, Tokai University, Japan; **James D. Dunn**, Tokai University, Japan; **Fergus Hann**, Tokai University, Japan; **Michael Hood**, Nihon University College of Commerce, Japan; **Hideyuki Kashimoto**, Shijonawate High School, Japan; **David Kennedy**, Nihon University, Japan; **Anna Youngna Kim**, Sogang University, South Korea; **Jae Phil Kim**, Sogang University, South Korea; **Jaganathan Krishnasamy**, GB Academy, Malaysia; **Peter Laver**, Incheon National University, South Korea; **Hung Hoang Le**, Ho Chi Minh City University of Technology, Vietnam; **Hyon Sook Lee**, Sogang University, South Korea; **Ji-seon Lee**, Iruda English Institute, South Korea; **Joo Young Lee**, Sogang University, South Korea; **Phung Tu Luc**, Ho Chi Minh City University of Technology, Vietnam; **Richard Mansbridge**, Hoa Sen University, Vietnam; **Kahoko Matsumoto**, Tokai University, Japan; **Elizabeth May**, Sangmyung University, South Korea; **Naoyuki Naganuma**, Tokai University, Japan; **Hiroko Nishikage**, Taisho University, Japan; **Yongjun Park**, Sangji University, South Korea; **Paul Rogers**, Dongguk University, South Korea; **Scott Schafer**, Inha University, South Korea; **Michael Schvaudner**, Tokai University, Japan; **Brendan Smith**, RMIT University, School of Languages and English, Vietnam; **Peter Snashall**, Huachiew Chalermprakiet University, Thailand; **Makoto Takeda**, Sendai Third Senior High School, Japan; **Peter Talley**, Mahidol University, Faculty of ICT, Thailand; **Byron Thigpen**, Sogang University, South Korea; **Junko Yamaai**, Tokai University, Japan; **Junji Yamada**, Taisho University, Japan; **Sayoko Yamashita**, Women's University, Japan; **Masami Yukimori**, Taisho University, Japan

Middle East and North Africa

Sajjad Ahmad, Taibah University, Saudi Arabia; **Basma Alansari**, Taibah University, Saudi Arabia; **Marwa Al-ashqar**, Taibah University, Saudi Arabia; **Dr. Rashid Al-Khawaldeh**, Taibah University, Saudi Arabia; **Mohamed Almohamed**, Taibah University, Saudi Arabia; **Dr Musaad Alrahaili**, Taibah University, Saudi Arabia; **Hala Al Sammar**, Kuwait University, Kuwait; **Ahmed Alshammari**, Taibah University, Saudi Arabia; **Ahmed Alshamy**, Taibah University, Saudi Arabia; **Doniazad sultan AlShraideh**, Taibah University, Saudi Arabia; **Sahar Amer**, Taibah University, Saudi Arabia; **Nabeela Azam**, Taibah University, Saudi Arabia; **Hassan Bashir**, Edex, Saudi Arabia; **Rachel Batchilder**, College of the North Atlantic, Qatar; **Nicole Cuddie**, Community College of Qatar, Qatar; **Mahdi Duris**, King Saud University, Saudi Arabia; **Ahmed Ege**, Institute of Public Administration, Saudi Arabia; **Magda Fadle**, Victoria College, Egypt; **Mohammed Hassan**, Taibah University, Saudi Arabia; **Tom Hodgson**, Community College of Qatar, Qatar; **Ayub Agbar Khan**, Taibah University, Saudi Arabia; **Cynthia Le Joncour**, Taibah University, Saudi Arabia; **Ruari Alexander MacLeod**, Community College of Qatar, Qatar; **Nasir Mahmood**, Taibah University, Saudi Arabia; **Duria Salih Mahmoud**, Taibah University, Saudi Arabia; **Ameera McKoy**, Taibah University, Saudi Arabia; **Chaker Mhamdi**, Buraimi University College, Oman; **Baraa Shiekh Mohamed**, Community College of Qatar, Qatar; **Abduleelah Mohammed**, Taibah University, Saudi Arabia; **Shumaila Nasir**, Taibah University, Saudi Arabia; **Kevin Onwordi**, Taibah University, Saudi Arabia; **Dr. Navid Rahmani**, Community College of Qatar, Qatar; **Dr. Sabah Salman Sabbah**, Community College of Qatar, Qatar; **Salih**, Taibah University, Saudi Arabia; **Verna Santos-Nafrada**, King Saud University, Saudi Arabia; **Gamal Abdelfattah Shehata**, Taibah University, Saudi Arabia; **Ron Stefan**, Institute of Public Administration, Saudi Arabia; **Dr. Saad Torki**, Imam Abdulrahman Bin Faisal University, Dammam, Saudi Arabia; **Silvia Yafai**, Applied Technology High School/Secondary Technical School, UAE; **Mahmood Zar**, Taibah University, Saudi Arabia; **Thouraya Zheni**, Taibah University, Saudi Arabia

Turkey

Sema Babacan, Istanbul Medipol University; **Bilge Çöllüoğlu Yakar**, Bilkent University; **Liana Corniel**, Koc University; **Savas Geylanioglu**, Izmir Bahcesehir Science and Technology College; **Öznur Güler**, Giresun University; **Selen Bilginer Halefoğlu**, Maltepe University; **Ahmet Konukoğlu**, Hasan Kalyoncu University; **Mehmet Salih Yoğun**, Gaziantep Hasan Kalyoncu University; **Fatih Yücel**, Beykent University

Europe

Amina Al Hashamia, University of Exeter, UK; **Irina Gerasimova**, Saint-Petersburg Mining University, Russia; **Jodi**, Las Dominicas, Spain; **Marina Khanykova**, School 179, Russia; **Oksana Postnikova**, Lingua Practica, Russia; **Nina Vasilchenko**, Soho-Bridge Language School, Russia

CRITICAL THINKING

The unique critical thinking approach of the *Q: Skills for Success* series has been further enhanced in the Third Edition. New features help you analyze, synthesize, and develop your ideas.

Unit question

The thought-provoking unit questions engage you with the topic and provide a critical thinking framework for the unit.

 UNIT QUESTION

How can colors be useful?

A. Discuss these questions with your classmates.

1. Why can wearing dark clothes at night be dangerous? Why do traffic police in some countries wear orange?

2. Imagine you want to paint your house. What color do you choose? Why?

3. Look at the photo. How is color useful to this animal?

Analysis

You can discuss your opinion of each listening text and analyze how it changes your perspective on the unit question.

 SAY WHAT YOU THINK

SYNTHESIZE Think about the unit video, Listening 1, and Listening 2 as you discuss the questions.

1. Many families in the world today have family members who live in different countries. How does this affect family life? What are the advantages and disadvantages?

2. How important is it to keep in touch with your larger family, that is aunts, uncles, cousins, grandparents, and so on?

3. Who has been an important person in your life? It might be a family member or other person. Why is the person important?

NEW! Critical Thinking Strategy with video

Each unit includes a Critical Thinking Strategy with activities to give you step-by-step guidance in critical analysis of texts. An accompanying instructional video (available on iQ Online) provides extra support and examples.

NEW! Bloom's Taxonomy

Pink activity headings integrate verbs from Bloom's Taxonomy to help you see how each activity develops critical thinking skills.

CRITICAL THINKING STRATEGY

Ranking

To **rank** means to put things in order using certain criteria. A **criterion** (plural *criteria*) is a standard that you use when you make a decision or form an opinion about someone or something. In some cases, the choice of criteria is up to you. For example, you can rank books from those you like most to those you like least. This would be useful when cleaning out your bookshelves. Sometimes we need to rank things based on more fact-based criteria. For example, restaurant rankings are often based on things like price, how clean they are, or service.

iQ PRACTICE Go online to watch the Critical Thinking Video and check your comprehension. *Practice > Unit 5 > Activity 9*

F. APPLY What makes you who you are? Think about ideas from Listening 1 and Listening 2. Then number the items from 1 to 6 in order of importance for you (1 = most important, 6 = least important). Remember that in this example, there are no right or wrong answers.

Rank	Items
	My family now
	My DNA
	My education
	The country I live in
	My family history
	Other life experiences

G. EXPLAIN Work with a partner and compare your answers. Are they similar or different? Explain your choices.

WORK WITH THE VIDEO

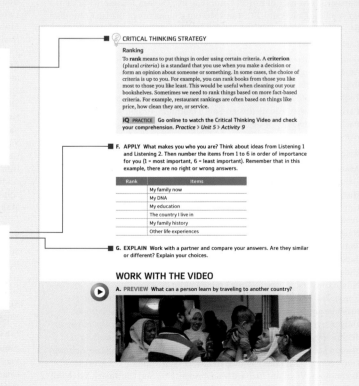 **A. PREVIEW** What can a person learn by traveling to another country?

THREE TYPES OF VIDEO

UNIT VIDEO

The unit videos include high-interest documentaries and reports on a wide variety of subjects, all linked to the unit topic and question.

NEW! "Work with the Video" pages guide you in watching, understanding, and discussing the unit videos. The activities help you see the connection to the Unit Question and the other texts in the unit.

NEW! In some units, one of the main listening texts is a video.

CRITICAL THINKING VIDEO

NEW! Narrated by the *Q* series authors, these short videos give you further instruction on the Critical Thinking Strategy of each unit using engaging images and graphics. You can use them to gain a deeper understanding of the Critical Thinking Strategy.

SKILLS VIDEO

NEW! These instructional videos provide illustrated explanations of skills and grammar points in the Student Book. They can be viewed in class or assigned for a flipped classroom, for homework, or for review. One skill video is available for every unit.

Easily access all videos in the Resources section of iQ Online.

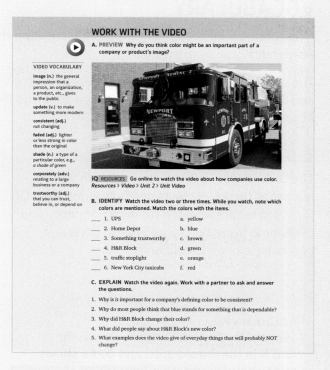

WORK WITH THE VIDEO

A. PREVIEW Why do you think color might be an important part of a company or product's image?

VIDEO VOCABULARY

image (n.) the general impression that a person, an organization, a product, etc., gives to the public

update (v.) to make something more modern

consistent (adj.) not changing

faded (adj.) lighter or less strong in color than the original

shade (n.) a type of a particular color, e.g., *a shade of green*

corporately (adv.) relating to a large business or a company

trustworthy (adj.) that you can trust, believe in, or depend on

iQ RESOURCES Go online to watch the video about how companies use color. *Resources > Video > Unit 2 > Unit Video*

B. IDENTIFY Watch the video two or three times. While you watch, note which colors are mentioned. Match the colors with the items.

____ 1. UPS   a. yellow
____ 2. Home Depot   b. blue
____ 3. Something trustworthy   c. brown
____ 4. H&R Block   d. green
____ 5. traffic stoplight   e. orange
____ 6. New York City taxicabs   f. red

C. EXPLAIN Watch the video again. Work with a partner to ask and answer the questions.

1. Why is it important for a company's defining color to be consistent?
2. Why do most people think that blue stands for something that is dependable?
3. Why did H&R Block change their color?
4. What did people say about H&R Block's new color?
5. What examples does the video give of everyday things that will probably NOT change?

How to compare and contrast

Venn Diagram

Firefighter — *fights fires* — *stays at the station until called*

Both — *help people* — *have dangerous jobs*

Police Officer — *fights crime* — *works on the street*

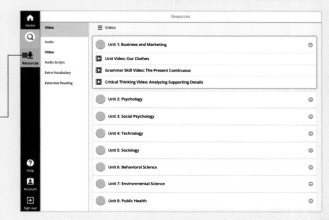

Resources

Video

Unit 1: Business and Marketing

Unit Video: Our Clothes

Grammar Skill Video: The Present Continuous

Critical Thinking Video: Analyzing Supporting Details

Unit 2: Psychology

Unit 3: Social Psychology

Unit 4: Technology

Unit 5: Sociology

Unit 6: Behavioral Science

Unit 7: Environmental Science

Unit 8: Public Health

VOCABULARY

A research-based vocabulary program focuses on the words you need to know academically and professionally.

The vocabulary syllabus in *Q: Skills for Success* is correlated to the CEFR (see page 184) and linked to two word lists: the Oxford 3000 and the OPAL (Oxford Phrasal Academic Lexicon).

⚵ OXFORD 3000

The Oxford 3000 lists the core words that every learner at the A1– B2 level needs to know. Items in the word list are selected for their frequency and usefulness from the Oxford English Corpus (a database of over 2 billion words).

Vocabulary Key
In vocabulary activities, ⚵ shows you the word is in the Oxford 3000 and **OPAL** shows you the word or phrase is in the OPAL.

OPAL
OXFORD PHRASAL ACADEMIC LEXICON

NEW! The OPAL is a collection of four word lists that provide an essential guide to the most important words and phrases to know for academic English. The word lists are based on the Oxford Corpus of Academic English and the British Academic Spoken English corpus. The OPAL includes both spoken and written academic English and both individual words and longer phrases.

Academic Language tips in the Student Book give information about how words and phrases from the OPAL are used and offer help with features such as collocations and phrases.

PREVIEW THE LISTENING

A. VOCABULARY Here are some words and phrases from Listening 2. Read the definitions. Then complete each sentence with the correct word or phrase.

attentive *(adjective)* watching or listening carefully
courteous *(adjective)* polite, having courtesy
deal with *(verb phrase)* to solve a problem
improve *(verb)* ⚵ OPAL to make something better
influence *(noun)* ⚵ OPAL the power to change how someone or something acts
principal *(noun)* the person in charge of a school
respect *(noun)* ⚵ OPAL consideration for the rights and feelings of other people
shout out *(verb phrase)* to say something in a loud voice
valuable *(adjective)* ⚵ OPAL very useful or important

⚵ Oxford 3000™ words   **OPAL** Oxford Phrasal Academic Lexicon

1. I apologized to show Sue I have _____ for her feelings.
2. The parents are meeting with the _____ tonight to discuss problems at school. She can make new school rules to stop the problems.

3. We need curtains on those windows. Without them, we have no _____ in the bedroom.

4. It is hard to discuss some things online. You need a _____ conversation where you can see the other person.

5. His _____ with Tom is very important to Reza. They have known each other for many years.

6. The newspaper _____ said that there will be bad snowstorms in the Midwest today.

7. Their family has lived here _____. I mean a very long time, more than 100 years.

8. The lecturer made some very _____ statements about social media. It gave me a lot to think about.

> **ACADEMIC LANGUAGE**
> The word *relationship* is often used in academic contexts. Notice that the suffix *-ship* is also used in the noun *friendship*. The suffix *-ship* indicates a state or condition.
>
> _____ **OPAL**
> Oxford Phrasal Academic Lexicon

iQ PRACTICE Go online for more practice with the vocabulary.
Practice > Unit 4 > Activities 3–4

B. PREVIEW You are going to listen to a lecture about social media and friendship. Work with a partner. List one good thing and one possible problem related to social media and friendships.

WORK WITH THE LISTENING

🔊 **A. LISTEN AND TAKE NOTES** Listen to Part 1 of the lecture. The speaker mentions three points that will be in the lecture. Prepare a piece of paper to take notes. List the three points and leave space for writing after each one.

EXTENSIVE READING

NEW! Extensive Reading is a program of reading for pleasure at a level that matches your language ability.

There are many benefits to Extensive Reading:

- It helps you to become a better reader in general.
- It helps to increase your reading speed.
- It can improve your reading comprehension.
- It increases your vocabulary range.
- It can help you improve your grammar and writing skills.
- It's great for motivation to read something that is interesting for its own sake.

Each unit of *Q: Skills for Success* Third Edition has been aligned to an Oxford Graded Reader based on the appropriate topic and level of language proficiency. The first chapter of each recommended graded reader can be downloaded from iQ Online Resources.

UNIT 1

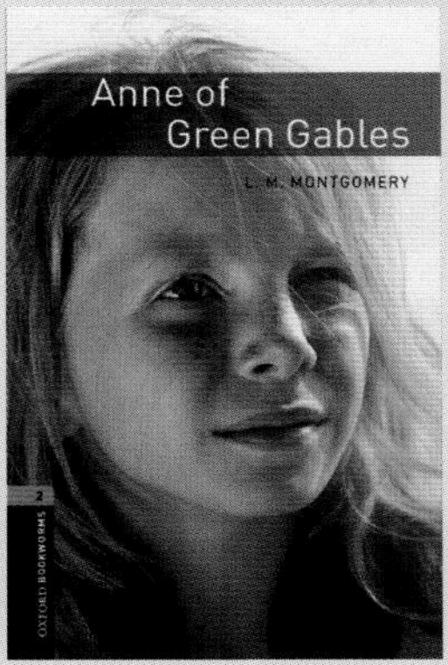

UNIT 2

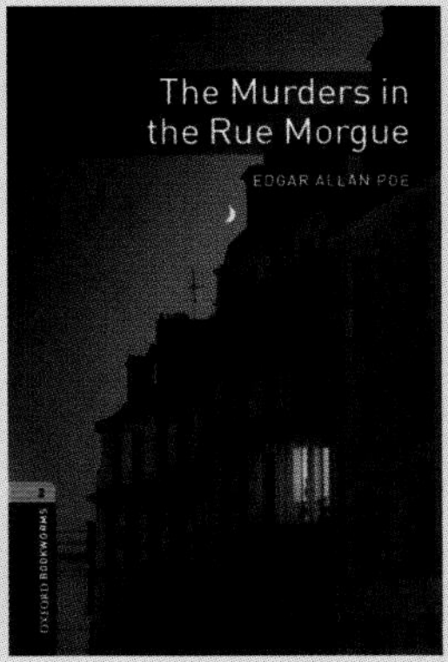

UNIT 3

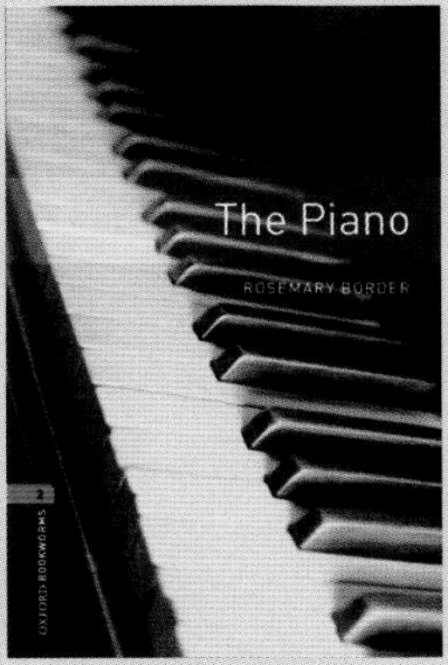

UNIT 4

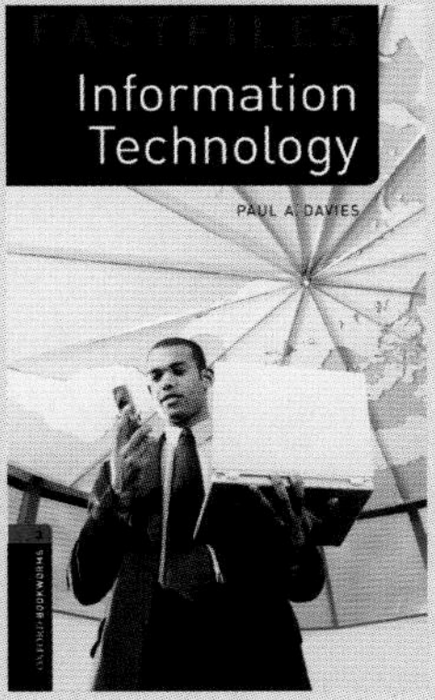

UNIT 5

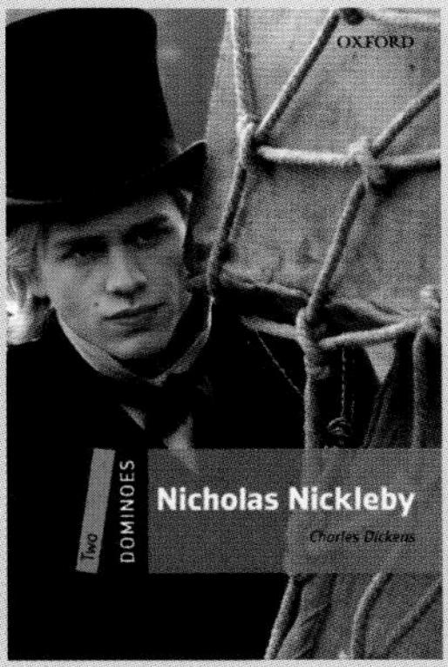

UNIT 6

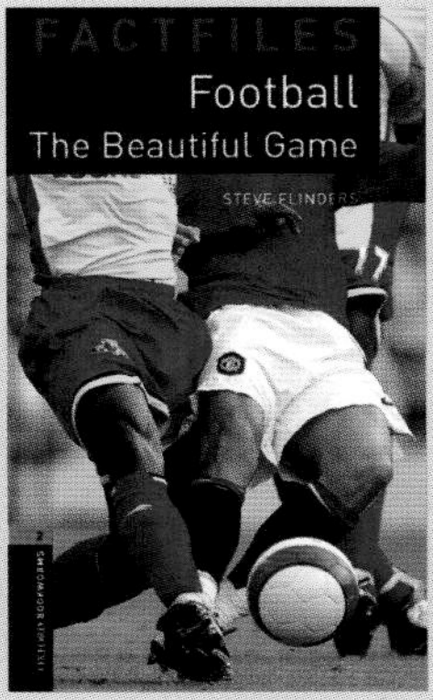

UNIT 7

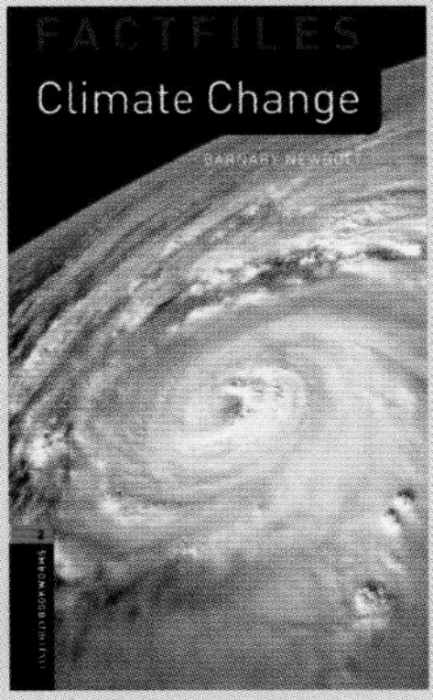

UNIT 8

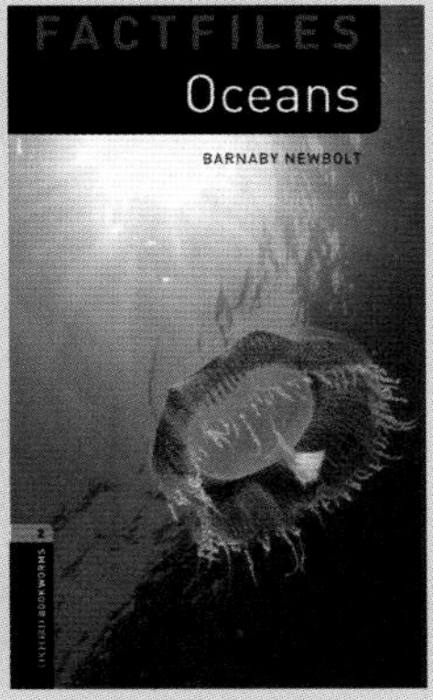

iQ ONLINE extends your learning beyond the classroom.

- Practice activities provide essential skills practice and support.
- Automatic grading and progress reports show you what you have mastered and where you need more practice.
- The Discussion Board allows you to discuss the Unit Questions and helps you develop your critical thinking.
- Essential resources such as audio and video are easy to access anytime.

NEW TO THE THIRD EDITION

- iQ Online is optimized for mobile use so you can use it on your phone.
- An updated interface allows easy navigation around the activities, tests, resources, and scores.
- New Critical Thinking Videos expand on the Critical Thinking Strategies in the Student Book.
- The Extensive Reading program helps you improve your vocabulary and reading skills.

How to use iQ ONLINE

Go to **Practice** to find additional practice and support to complement your learning in the classroom.

Go to **Resources** to find:
- All Student Book video
- All Student Book audio
- Critical Thinking videos
- Skills videos
- Extensive Reading

Go to **Messages** and **Discussion Board** to communicate with your teacher and classmates.

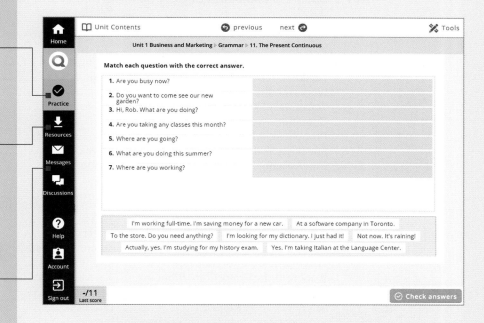

Online tests assigned by your teacher help you assess your progress and see where you need more practice.

A progress bar shows you how many activities you have completed.

View your scores for all activities.

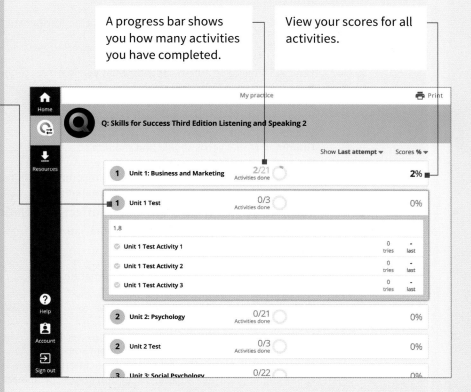

CONTENTS

Business and Marketing

NOTE-TAKING	identifying key words
LISTENING	listening for main ideas
CRITICAL THINKING	analyzing supporting details
VOCABULARY	collocations: nouns and verbs
GRAMMAR	the present continuous
PRONUNCIATION	interjections and intonation
SPEAKING	drawing attention to main ideas

How important is it to keep up with current trends?

A. Discuss these questions with your classmates.

1. What are some of the latest trends in your community? Think about things like clothing, food, and technology.

2. How do these trends affect the way people live, use technology, or shop?

3. Look at the photo. Why are these people waiting in line?

B. Listen to *The Q Classroom* online. Then answer these questions.

1. How important does Sophy think it is to keep up with the latest changes in technology?

2. Do Marcus and Yuna agree with Sophy? Why or why not?

3. How is Felix's response different from that of the others?

iQ PRACTICE Go to the online discussion board to discuss the Unit Question with your classmates. *Practice > Unit 1 > Activity 1*

UNIT OBJECTIVE ▶ Listen to a podcast and a conversation. Gather information and ideas to create a survey about trends.

When you take notes, write only *key* words—the most important words. Don't spend time writing little words like *of, the, and,* etc. Here are some ways to identify key words as you listen:

- Listen for repeated words. These often point to the main idea.

- Focus on words that the speaker defines. If a speaker takes time to say what a word means, it's probably important.

- Listen for words the speaker emphasizes by saying them more slowly or a little louder.

A. IDENTIFY Read the beginning of a lecture about the difference between a trend and a fad. Underline words that you think are important. The word *fad* is underlined as an example.

To be successful in business, it is important to be able to tell the difference between a <u>fad</u> and a trend. A fad is something that becomes popular quite suddenly but does not last very long. A trend is the general direction in which something is developing or growing. In business, following a trend usually leads to more success than chasing after a fad. Trying to make money on a fad is risky.

B. APPLY Listen as the speaker continues the lecture. Identify important words as you hear them and take notes. Does the speaker repeat any of the words you underlined in Activity A?

C. DISCUSS Compare notes with a partner. Which words did you underline? Why?

iQ PRACTICE Go online for more practice identifying key words while taking notes. *Practice > Unit 1 > Activity 2*

LISTENING 1

OBJECTIVE ▶

They Said It Was Just a Fad

[handwritten: trend]

You are going to listen to a podcast about inventions that some people thought were just fads. As you listen, gather information and ideas about the importance of keeping up with current trends.

[handwritten: put break in something " stop]

[handwritten: Decline (v) " to say "No"]

[handwritten: Decline (v) " go down]

PREVIEW THE LISTENING

[handwritten: 1 2 5 7 8]

[handwritten: Important = not nessesary]

A. VOCABULARY Here are some words from Listening 1. Read the sentences. Then match each <u>underlined</u> word with its definition on page 6.

[handwritten: nessecary essential (need to live)]

___d___ 1. That popular restaurant chain has to make a lot of money. The person who started it must be very <u>wealthy</u> now.

___a___ 2. During the winter months here, it is <u>essential</u> to have a warm coat. It gets very cold!

___g___ 3. I need to get the <u>brakes</u> on my car fixed. I'm having problems stopping.

___b___ 4. Sales of the toys went up in November and December, but they <u>declined</u> in January.

___c___ 5. Our attempt to build a robot was a complete <u>failure</u>. It just didn't work at all.

___e___ 6. My daughter loves that song that says, "The <u>wheels</u> on the bus go round and round." I'm tired of hearing it!

___h___ 7. They live in an <u>enormous</u> house. It has six bedrooms.

___f___ 8. Now, that car is way too expensive, but this smaller one is quite <u>affordable</u>.

[handwritten: They can not afford to buy / It's unaffordable to but"]
[handwritten: unaffordable]

ACADEMIC LANGUAGE

The verb *decline* is common in spoken and written academic English. It is often used with adverbs that describe the degree of the decline: for example, *decline significantly | slowly | rapidly*.

⌐ OPAL
Oxford Phrasal Academic Lexicon

a. *(adjective)* completely necessary
b. *(verb)* to become smaller, fewer, or less
c. *(noun)* a person or thing that is unsuccessful
d. *(adjective)* having a lot of money and property
e. *(noun)* round objects under a car or other vehicle that turn when it moves
f. *(adjective)* not expensive; cheap enough for most people to be able to buy
g. *(noun)* the parts of a car or other vehicle that make it go slower or stop
h. *(adjective)* very large

iQ PRACTICE   Go online for more practice with the vocabulary.
Practice > Unit 1 > Activities 3–4

B. PREVIEW You are going to listen to a podcast called *They Said It Was Just a Fad*. It describes three inventions that people thought were just fads and would never be used to create a successful business. Work with a partner. What key words do you think you will hear? Make a list.

WORK WITH THE LISTENING

A. LISTEN AND TAKE NOTES Listen to the podcast. Write any key words you hear. Leave space on the page to add more notes later. Here are some words to get you started.

costlecs

Lightbulb	for mantions	cheat	candle
Edison	light compay	welthy	
affordable	way of future	foter faviler	
change lives	hive	new	
f	New thinv dei	brake — no tuive	
Bicycle	trend s	esay ridu	transportation
toppy	imierstn	saftybike 60	cost ress
Fidget spinner	wo we	play aroud	

boring → stresfull   trial toy △

2017   not jost fad

neuvoug energy

yuv wissit

B. EXTEND Listen again. Add more information to your notes.

C. ANALYZE Check (✓) the two statements that express the main ideas in the podcast.

✓ 1. Some things that people thought were just fads became successful businesses in the end.

___ 2. A business based on a fad, like fidget spinners, will always lose money.

✓ 3. It sometimes takes a long time before you know if something will last or if it is just a fad.

D. EXPLAIN Answer the questions. Then listen and check your answers.

TIP FOR SUCCESS

Many students are nervous about listening. Take a deep breath and relax! If you are nervous or stressed, it's more difficult to listen and understand what you hear.

1. What did J. P. Morgan do to show that he believed in Edison's lightbulbs?
   light is way of future   400 installed for mantions in NY

2. What did Morgan's father think about the idea of having electric light?
   He thout It was food   never last   wheels
                                                              size op

3. Why were the early bicycles called *velocipedes* dangerous to ride?
   dificult to controle / NO brakes   there are diffrence

4. How were "safety" bicycles different from velocipedes?
   have breats (same size wheele) / smaller than privous one

5. Did bicycle use decline after more people had cars?
   car appear   (Yos)

6. Why have bicycles been a successful area of business for so many years?
   esy to drive / sport / trasportation / NO fuail

7. What is a fidget spinner, and what is it used for?
   a litle   bored / nervous / play their finger

8. Does the speaker say whether the spinners are a fad or a lasting trend? Why or why not?
   _our
   deal with stress   no desturing people_

LISTENING 1 **7**

E. IDENTIFY Which invention does each comment below apply to? Mark each as *L* (lightbulb), *B* (bicycle), or *F* (fidget spinner).

_L_ 1. One inventor thought making it affordable would change people's lives.

_F_ 2. This trend "is ending and you missed it!"

_L_ 3. A scientist described it as a complete failure.

_L_ 4. Now "only the rich will burn candles."

_B_ 5. In 1902, one newspaper said that as a fad, the activity was dead.

_F_ 6. They "are not just a fad" because they help people deal with stressful situations.

F. CATEGORIZE Read the words and phrases in the word box. Write the words associated with each item in the appropriate column of the chart.

~~affordable~~   brakes   candles   cheap electricity
fuel   nervous energy   play around   transportation
triangular toy   wheels

Lightbulb	Bicycle	Fidget spinner
affordable Candles cheap electricity	brakes Wheels transportaion	tringular toy

iQ PRACTICE Go online for additional listening and comprehension.
Practice > Unit 1 > Activity 5

SAY WHAT YOU THINK

DISCUSS Discuss the questions in a small group.

1. Think of a fad that is no longer popular, such as pet rocks. How long did it last? Why did it die out? Furby

2. What is something that is newly popular in your community now? Is it a fad or a trend? Why?

3. A friend of yours wants to start a business selling robot fish as "pets." These are mechanical fish. You put them in water and they "swim" around. Will this be a fad or a trend? Will it be successful? Explain.

The **main idea** is the most important thing the speaker wants you to understand. Speakers often use several strategies to emphasize their main idea. Listen for repeated words and ideas. Listen for emphasis on certain words or sentences. Also listen for speakers to summarize the main ideas at the end of their talk.

A. ANALYZE Listen to a report from a panel discussion about the future of food. Check (✓) the sentence that best states the main idea of the report.

____ 1. In the future, the food industry needs to be entirely focused on vegetarian choices.

____ 2. People say they want healthier foods, but in fact they buy a lot of foods that aren't good for them.

____ 3. The movement toward having healthier foods with clear labels will continue.

B. INTERPRET Look at these words from the listening.

1. Are there any you did not hear or understand? Circle them.

available	bother	brand	cuisine
evident	entrepreneur	fertilizer	grocery
hummus	transparency		

2. Why was it possible to understand the main idea without knowing all of these words?

3. What words or ideas did the speaker repeat or emphasize? How did they help you understand the main idea?

iQ PRACTICE Go online for more practice listening for main ideas.
Practice > Unit 1 > Activity 6

CRITICAL THINKING STRATEGY

Analyzing supporting details

It is important to analyze the details and examples that a speaker uses to support his or her main ideas. If an idea is not supported well, listeners will think the idea has no value. Ask: *Does this example support the main idea?* In some cases, the answer might be that it doesn't. Look at these examples.

Main idea: The trend toward healthier foods is going to continue.

Example: Shoppers spend a lot every year on sodas and sweet treats.

This example doesn't support the main idea. In fact, it says the opposite. The speaker uses it to present another side of the issue.

Main idea: The bicycle was a fad that became a trend.

Example: Today, people in cities all around the world use bicycles for transportation.

This example supports the main idea by showing that bicycles continue to be popular.

iQ PRACTICE   Go online to watch the Critical Thinking Video and check your comprehension. *Practice > Unit 1 > Activity 7*

C. ANALYZE Choose the example that <u>best</u> supports each main idea.

1. Sometimes hard work and a strong belief can make an invention successful.

   a. Today, many things we use every day depend on electricity.

   b. J. P. Morgan's father thought that Edison's ideas wouldn't work and that electricity was just a fad.

   c. Edison believed that electricity would change lives, so he installed 400 lightbulbs in Morgan's home.

2. It's too soon to tell whether the fidget spinner is a fad or a trend.

   a. The popularity of other inventions often increased and decreased over time.

   b. With the spinner, people can fidget in boring meetings and not disturb others.

   c. Many people think spinners help people reduce stress levels.

3. A successful bookstore has to be more than just a place to buy books.

   a. Children's bookstores continue to be successful.

   b. Corner Store Books invited the local chess club to meet at the store.

   c. There are fewer shoppers downtown these days because so many stores are closing.

D. EXPLAIN Work with a partner. Compare your answers in Activity A and explain your choices.

LISTENING 2   Bucking the Trend

OBJECTIVE ▶

You are going to listen to a conversation between two friends, Asha and Kim. Asha wants to open a new business. As you listen, gather information and ideas about the importance of keeping up with current trends.

PREVIEW THE LISTENING

A. VOCABULARY Here are some words and phrases from Listening 2. Read the definitions. Then complete each sentence with the correct word or phrase.

---

advertise *(verb)* 🔑 to publish information to persuade people to buy something

buck the trend *(verb phrase)* to do something that goes against what is currently popular or fashionable

chat *(verb)* 🔑 to talk to someone in a friendly, informal way

get the point *(verb phrase)* to understand the main idea of something

postage *(noun)* the amount of money it costs to send a letter, package, etc.

potential *(adjective)* 🔑 OPAL that may possibly become something

realize *(verb)* 🔑 to come to understand that something is true

reasonable *(adjective)* 🔑 OPAL not too expensive

🔑 Oxford 3000™ words   **OPAL** Oxford Phrasal Academic Lexicon

1. I'm sorry I don't have time to ___chat___ right now. Let's talk later; I have to leave for an appointment.

2. They want $5,000 for their car. I think that's a ___reasonable___ price.

3. He talked for an hour, but I still didn't _____. What was he trying to say?
   ___get the point___

4. What's the _____postage_____ to mail a letter to Canada?

5. If you want your store to be successful, you have to ___*advertise*___. If you don't, no one will know it's here.

6. They're interviewing two ___*potential*___ candidates for the job. Jay thinks either of them will work well with our team.

7. Jack always tries to ___*buck the trend*___. He wants to be different from everyone else.

8. I didn't _____ (*realizes*) that e-books were so popular! I'm happy to learn that.

iQ PRACTICE Go online for more practice with the vocabulary.
Practice > Unit 1 > Activities 8–9

B. PREVIEW You're going to listen to *Bucking the Trend*, a conversation between two people, Asha and Kim. Asha wants to buy and run a bookstore, like some other stores that are "bucking the trend." Kim thinks it may be risky. What problems could there be with this plan? Discuss with a partner.

WORK WITH THE LISTENING

A. LISTEN AND TAKE NOTES Listen to the conversation. First, prepare a note page with two columns labeled *Pro* and *Con*. *Pro* is for arguments that support starting a bookstore business. *Con* is for arguments against it. As you listen, write key words in each column. Leave space to add to your notes later.

Pro (*Possitve*)	Con (*Negatve*)
independent	risky
small *increase* *enjoy*	*few* *ungoing*
quick *comportable* *friendly*	*tired* *buck the trend*
crazy	*book with closing*

B. EXTEND Listen again. Add more information to your notes.

C. EVALUATE Compare notes with a partner. Correct and edit your notes as needed.

D. IDENTIFY Read the questions. Choose the correct answers.

1. Which of these is NOT a reason Asha gives for wanting to open a bookstore?

   a. She likes to read print books instead of e-books.

   b. She wants to work for herself, not for other people.

   c. She saw a bookstore for sale nearby at a good price.

2. Why does Kim think Asha's plan might be risky?

    a. Fewer people are reading books now.

    b. Bookstores are gathering places for people in the community.

    c. People nowadays are buying more books online, not in stores.

3. What has Asha's research shown her?

    a. She should open a store just for children's books.

    b. Small, independent bookstores can be successful.

    c. People are now buying more e-books than print books.

4. What does Kim like about shopping in bookstores?

    a. Stores are less crowded than they used to be.

    b. She can buy a book and take it home right away.

    c. She doesn't have to talk to people while she's shopping.

E. EXPLAIN Work with a partner. The graph below shows the percentage of book purchases that were e-books from 2012 to 2016. Answer the questions.

1. Which category had the highest percentage of e-book sales in all five years? Why do you think this is so?

2. Which category had the lowest percentage of e-book sales? How can you explain this?

3. How do nonfiction e-book sales compare to fiction e-book sales?

4. How can you describe the trend toward e-book sales between 2012 and 2016?

5. Do these statistics support Asha's idea that she can "buck the trend" toward e-books and open a bookstore? Why or why not?

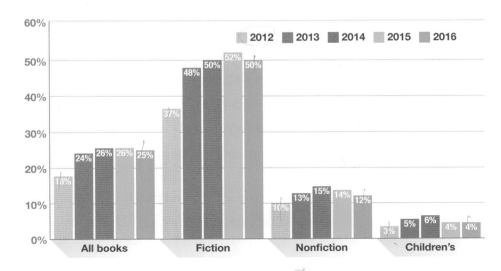

WORK WITH THE VIDEO

A. PREVIEW What do you do with clothes that you can't or don't want to wear anymore? Do you prefer traditional clothing or modern clothing?

iQ RESOURCES Go online to watch the video about trends in clothing in Ghana. *Resources > Video > Unit 1 > Unit Video*

B. INTERPRET Choose the correct answers.

1. Where does most of the clothing in the market come from?
   a. Africa
   b. China
   c. Europe

2. What does the woman say about the piece of clothing she is looking at?
   a. It's too expensive.
   b. It's the best quality.
   c. It's in bad condition.

3. What does the historian say about traditional clothing?
   a. In the past, people used traditional clothing to tell the history of the country.
   b. It's cheaper than secondhand clothing from Europe and America.
   c. People will always want to wear traditional clothing.

4. What does the woman in the city say about traditional and European clothing?

   a. Traditional clothing was popular a couple of years ago, but it isn't popular now.

   b. Traditional clothing is now "cooler," more popular, than European clothing.

   c. She prefers to wear European clothing when she goes out.

C. EXPLAIN Watch the video again. Discuss the questions in a small group.

1. Why do you think traditional clothing is more expensive than secondhand clothing in Ghana? *It still makes by traditionl way . and takes time.*

2. Is it important for countries to keep their traditional clothing styles? Why or why not? *Yes , becase if Noone wear them they will desapear.*

 # SAY WHAT YOU THINK

SYNTHESIZE Think about the unit video, Listening 1, and Listening 2 as you discuss the questions.

1. How do you feel about buying secondhand clothing? What other things do people sometimes buy secondhand?

2. Like traditional Ghanaian clothing, some things go out of style for a time and then come back. What things can you think of that were out of style for a time but are popular now?

3. Describe a time in your life when you decided to "buck a trend"—that is, do something your own way, not following what others were doing. Was it a successful experience? Why or why not?

VOCABULARY SKILL Collocations: nouns and verbs

Collocations are groups of words that are commonly used together. One type of collocation is the combination of a **verb + noun**.

The word web shows verbs often used with the noun *risk*.

take a risk

take
Sometimes you have to **take a risk**.

take a

risk

reduce
Eating less sugar will **reduce your risk** of getting sick.

Reduce a risk

run the risk

run
If you drive too fast, you **run the risk** of having an accident.

involve
Practicing a sport always **involves some risk**.

involve a risk

A. IDENTIFY Read the sentences. Underline each verb used as a collocation with the noun *trend*.

1. Hey, your shoes look cool! I'm going to get some, too. We can start a trend.

2. Franco doesn't like to follow architectural trends. His buildings follow a classical style.

3. I wasn't trying to set a new trend in transportation. I ride my bike to work because the bus schedule doesn't work for me.

4. More and more people are driving cars, even for short distances. I want to buck this trend and start walking everywhere I go.

5. Buildings in my city are getting more energy efficient. I hope architects continue this trend.

B. APPLY Complete the word web. Use the words you underlined in Activity A.

set a trend
" "
2 " "trendsetter"

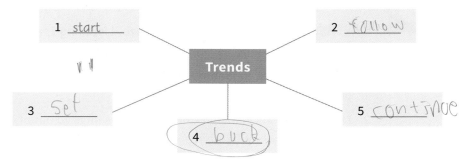

1 __start__

2 __follow__

Trends

3 __set__

4 __buck__

5 __continue__

iQ PRACTICE Go online for more practice using noun-verb collocations.
Practice > Unit 1 > Activity 10

SPEAKING

OBJECTIVE ▶

At the end of this unit, you are going to work in a group to do some "trend spotting" and then present your findings to the class. As you speak, you will need to highlight your main ideas.

GRAMMAR The present continuous

We use the **present continuous** to describe actions taking place at the moment of speaking. Look at this example from Listening 2. It describes what Asha is doing at that moment.

Kim: What are you doing?
Asha: I'm calling the agent for the store.

We can also use the present continuous to describe actions taking place around but not exactly at the moment of speaking. These actions continue for a period of time. Look at this sentence from Listening 2. It describes a trend that is continuing into the future.

Statistics show that people **are still buying** more print books than e-books.

How to form the present continuous:

Affirmative

Use a form of *be* + verb + *-ing*

She **is buying** a book now.

Negative

Use the word *not* before the *-ing* verb (*be* + *not* + verb + *-ing*).

He **is not using** his car to go to work this week.

iQ RESOURCES Go online to watch the Grammar Skill Video.
Resources > Video > Unit 1 > Grammar Skill Video

A. COMPOSE Write sentences with the present continuous. Then read your sentences to a partner.

1. Sales / independent bookstores / increase / all the time

   Sales independent bookstores are increasing all the time

2. Everyone / wear / red these days / because it's a trendy color!

   Everyone is wearing read thesd days, because

   it's a trendy color.

Everyone is one group

3. We / discuss / the difference / between a fad and a trend

  We're discussing the diffrence between a fan & a trend

4. More people / ride / bicycles / to work these days

  More people are riding bicydes to work these days

B. **ANALYZE** Listen to the conversations. Decide whether each describes actions that are happening now or actions that are happening around now. Check (✓) the correct answer.

	Happening now	Happening around now
1.	☑	☐
2.	☐	☑
3.	☐	☑
4.	☑	☐
5.	☐	☑
6.	☐	☑

iQ PRACTICE Go online for more practice with the present continuous. *Practice > Unit 1 > Activity 11*

iQ PRACTICE Go online for the Grammar Expansion: present continuous and simple present. *Practice > Unit 1 > Activity 12*

Interjections are short words, phrases, or sounds that people use when they speak. Interjections often express feelings. For example, *Wow!* is an interjection that usually indicates surprise or excitement.

⌈ **Wow!** That was a quick decision.

The meaning of an interjection often depends on the speaker's **intonation**. For example, *Oh!* can express different emotions, as in these examples.

⌈ **Oh!** Look at all the customers coming into the store! (happiness)

Oh! Our sales declined again this month. (disappointment)

Oh! Someone parked in front of the driveway. Now we can't get into the garage! (anger)

Sometimes speakers use an interjection just to give themselves time to think. Sounds like *hmm* and *uh* are used in this way.

⌈ **Hmm.** I know what you mean.

EVALUATE Listen to the sentences. The same speaker will read each one twice with different intonation. Answer the questions. Check (✓) the correct answer.

1. Well, I think this is the right answer.

   Which sentence sounds less sure?

   ____ 1   ✓ 2

2. Yeah, and after we finish this project, we're going to do another one.

   Which sentence sounds more excited?

   ____ 1   ✓ 2

3. Yeah, I lost my presentation.

Which sentence sounds more disappointed?

___ 1   _✓_ 2

4. Oh! Mr. Lombardi is going to be in Tokyo next week.

Which sentence sounds happier?

_✓_ 1   ___ 2

iQ PRACTICE Go online for more practice with interjections and intonation.
Practice > Unit 1 > Activity 13

SPEAKING SKILL Drawing attention to main ideas

When you speak, help listeners understand your main ideas.

- Repeat an important idea with different words.

  Morgan's father thought electric light was just a fad. **In other words,** he thought it wouldn't last.

- Use phrases for emphasis.

  The point is that many people *enjoy* going to bookstores.

- Summarize the main ideas of the presentation.

  To sum up, it isn't always easy to start something completely new.

A. DISCUSS Work in a small group. Choose one of the following statements and discuss it for one minute. Give examples and draw attention to the main ideas. Take turns.

1. [Your own idea] is just a fad. It will never last.

2. Electricity was one of the most important discoveries of all time.

3. Twenty years from now there will be more (or no more) bookstores.

B. DISCUSS Listen to the other members of your group. Note the expressions that people use as they give examples and draw attention to their main idea. Discuss your notes with the group.

iQ PRACTICE Go online for more practice with drawing attention to main ideas. *Practice > Unit 1 > Activity 14*

UNIT ASSIGNMENT

OBJECTIVE ▶

An experiment with trend spotting →

In this section, you are going to work with a small group to conduct an experiment with "trend spotting." You will conduct a survey using your classmates as your subjects and then present your findings to the class. As you prepare your presentation, think about the Unit Question, "How important is it to keep up with current trends?" Use information from Listening 1, Listening 2, the unit video, and your work in this unit to support your presentation. Refer to the Self-Assessment checklist on page 22.

CONSIDER THE IDEAS

INVESTIGATE Listen to Uma and Dareen's discussion about trend spotting. Answer the questions.

1. What is trend spotting?

2. What is one example of a way in which people use trend spotting?

3. What is a survey?

4. How does Uma feel about the focus on trends? Do you agree? Explain.

PREPARE AND SPEAK

A. GATHER IDEAS Work with a small group. Prepare your trend spotting experiment.

1. Choose a subject from the list below or use your own idea.

Trends in:
• Clothing
• Food
• Technology
• Books
• Transportation

2. Prepare a survey question or questions for your classmates about the topic you have chosen.

3. Conduct the survey. Talk to your classmates and take notes about their answers.

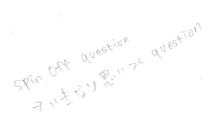

spin off question
ついでなり聞いつく question

B. **ORGANIZE IDEAS** With your group, discuss the answers you receive and plan your presentation.

1. Summarize the responses to your survey in a chart.

2. Plan the presentation, making sure each person has a role to play. What were the results of the survey? If you were a business person, how could you use this information? How did you feel about the activity?

C. **SPEAK** Practice your presentation. Then give your presentation to the class or in a small group. Refer to the Self-Assessment checklist below before you begin.

iQ PRACTICE Go online for your alternate Unit Assignment.
Practice > Unit 1 > Activity 15

CHECK AND REFLECT

A. **CHECK** Think about the Unit Assignment as you complete the Self-Assessment checklist.

SELF-ASSESSMENT	Yes	No
I was able to speak easily about the topic.	☐	☐
My group or class understood me.	☐	☐
I used the present continuous correctly.	☐	☐
I used vocabulary from the unit.	☐	☐
I drew attention to the main ideas.	☐	☐
I used intonation to express feelings.	☐	☐
I analyzed supporting details.	☐	☐

B. **REFLECT** Discuss these questions with a partner or group.

1. What is something new you learned in this unit?

2. Look back at the Unit Question—How important is it to keep up with current trends? Is your answer different now than when you started this unit? If yes, how is it different? Why?

iQ PRACTICE Go to the online discussion board to discuss the questions.
Practice > Unit 1 > Activity 16

TRACK YOUR SUCCESS

iQ PRACTICE Go online to check the words and phrases you have learned in this unit. *Practice > Unit 1 > Activity 17*

Check (✓) the skills and strategies you learned. If you need more work on a skill, refer to the page(s) in parentheses.

NOTE-TAKING	☐ I can identify key words. (p. 4)
LISTENING	☐ I can listen for main ideas. (p. 9)
CRITICAL THINKING	☐ I can analyze supporting details. (p. 10)
VOCABULARY	☐ I can recognize and use noun and verb collocations. (p. 15)
GRAMMAR	☐ I can use the present continuous. (p. 17)
PRONUNCIATION	☐ I can use interjections and intonation. (p. 19)
SPEAKING	☐ I can draw attention to main ideas. (p. 20)
OBJECTIVE ▶	☐ I can gather information and ideas to make a presentation about a current trend.

2 Psychology

How can colors be useful?

A. Discuss these questions with your classmates.

1. Why can wearing dark clothes at night be dangerous? Why do traffic police in some countries wear orange?

2. Imagine you want to paint your house. What color do you choose? Why?

3. Look at the photo. How is color useful to this animal?

B. Listen to *The Q Classroom* online. Then match the ideas in the box to the students in the chart.

a. to affect moods	e. different-colored notebooks
b. ~~for symbolic reasons~~	f. to organize
c. hospitals use relaxing colors	g. wearing school colors
d. to attract attention	h. big red letters on a sign

	Use of color	Example
Sophy	*b. for symbolic reasons*	
Felix		
Marcus		
Yuna		

iQ PRACTICE Go to the online discussion board to discuss the Unit Question with your classmates. *Practice > Unit 2 > Activity 1*

UNIT OBJECTIVE

Listen to a nature program and a panel presentation. Gather information and ideas to give a presentation about the uses of color.

Instructors often use visual elements in their classes. They sometimes refer to pictures in a textbook or show photographs and charts on a screen. They also draw simple pictures and diagrams on the board. To use a visual element in your notes, you can . . .

- first copy the picture or diagram into your notes.

- then label the picture and write notes around it.

You don't need to be a great artist to use pictures in your notes. Even a rough drawing will help you remember the contents of the class.

A. IDENTIFY Look at the picture of a leaf used in a biology class and read the instructor's explanation. Then finish labeling the student's drawing and write notes.

The Structure of a Leaf

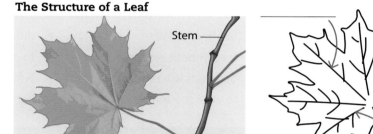

The leaves are the food-making part of a plant. The *petiole* connects the leaf to a *stem* on the plant. The petiole is like a small tube or pipe. It carries water and minerals to the leaf. Water goes from the petiole to the *midrib*. The midrib runs from the bottom to the top of the leaf. Then small *veins* distribute this water all through the leaf. The petiole also turns the leaf toward the sun. This is important because leaves use energy from the sun to make food from carbon dioxide in the air and water. This process is called *photosynthesis*.

B. APPLY Look at the picture of the tree. Make a drawing of it. Then listen as an instructor describes the parts of a tree and make notes.

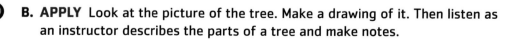

iQ PRACTICE Go online for more practice using visual elements in your notes. *Practice > Unit 2 > Activity 2*

Parts of a tree

LISTENING 1

OBJECTIVE ▶

The Colors of Nature

You are going to listen to part of a nature program. A famous scientist talks about how animals use color. As you listen, gather information and ideas about how colors can be useful.

PREVIEW THE LISTENING

A. VOCABULARY Here are some words from Listening 1. Read the sentences. Then choose the answer that best matches the meaning of each underlined word.

1. Animals <u>hide</u> when danger is near. They come out when it's safe.

   a. go to a place where no one can see them

   b. come out and look around

2. Listen to that bird. I think it's giving the other birds a <u>warning</u> that there's a cat hunting them.

   a. a call that means hunger

   b. a call that means danger

3. Don't let the children touch that. It is rat <u>poison</u>. It can hurt them.

   a. something that is dangerous to touch or eat

   b. something that has a very bad taste

4. This hand cream makes your <u>skin</u> soft and beautiful.

   a. outer covering of your body

   b. shoes and clothing

5. Some large birds have <u>wings</u> that are more than six feet across.

   a. body parts used to walk

   b. body parts used to fly

6. Most pets can't <u>survive</u> in the wild. They need people to take care of them.

   a. stay alive

   b. find friends

7. Lions are <u>predators</u>. Other animals stay away from lions because they are dangerous.

   a. animals that live in a group

   b. animals that kill and eat other animals

8. All <u>insects</u> have six legs, and many have wings. Most are very small.

   a. an animal like an ant or a bee

   b. an animal like a cat or a rabbit

iQ PRACTICE   Go online for more practice with the vocabulary.
Practice > Unit 2 > Activities 3–4

B. PREVIEW You are going to listen to a nature program about ways animals use color. Work with a partner. Discuss these questions.

1. Look at photos 1 and 2. Why is it difficult to see the animals in these photos?

2. Look at photo 3. Is it easy or difficult to see the frog?

3. Why do you think the animals have these colors?

A false-leaf katydid

A cryptic frog

A blue poison dart frog

WORK WITH THE LISTENING

A. INVESTIGATE Look at the photos again. Make rough sketches of the animals on a page for your notes. Label the photos and make notes about what you see—for example, color, size, or location. Leave room on the page to add more information.

B. LISTEN AND TAKE NOTES Listen to the nature program and take more notes about each animal in the photos.

C. CATEGORIZE Complete the chart with the words in the box. Then listen and check your answers.

among the green leaves	blue	brown
on the forest floor	green	in the rain forest

	False-leaf katydid	Cryptic frog	Poison dart frog
Color			
Location			

D. IDENTIFY Read the sentences. Then listen again. Choose the answer that best completes each statement.

1. The false-leaf katydid's ____ look just like leaves.

    a. eyes   b. wings   c. legs

2. The katydid gets its name from ____.

    a. a girl named Katy   b. the way it looks   c. a sound it makes

3. The colors of the cryptic frog match the leaves and ____ on the forest floor.

    a. rocks   b. insects   c. flowers

4. The best way to see a cryptic frog is to ____.

    a. wait for the wind   b. watch for it to move   c. look under a rock
       to blow

5. The blue poison dart frog has enough poison to kill ____.

    a. one person   b. five people   c. ten people

6. Poison dart frogs live in the rain forests of ____.

    a. South America   b. South Africa   c. North America

E. EXPLAIN Work with a partner. Take turns asking and answering the questions. Use your own words.

1. What does the word *camouflage* mean? Why do animals use camouflage?

2. How does the poison dart frog use color? How is it different from the cryptic frog?

F. CATEGORIZE Read the descriptions of these animals. Do you think they use color for camouflage or as a warning? Write *C* (camouflage) or *W* (warning). Compare answers with a partner.

_____ 1. Monarch butterflies are bright orange. Their wings have a terrible taste.

_____ 2. Zebras are African animals in the horse family. They have black and white stripes. You often find them standing in tall grass.

_____ 3. The coral snake lives in forests. It has red, yellow, and black stripes.

_____ 4. The arctic fox has brown or gray fur in the summer, but in winter its fur changes to white.

iQ PRACTICE Go online for additional listening and comprehension.
Practice > Unit 2 > Activity 5

SAY WHAT YOU THINK

DISCUSS Discuss the questions in a group.

1. Think about the animals in Activity D on page 29. Do these animals use color for camouflage or as a warning? Explain.

2. Most large predators, like lions, are not brightly colored. Why do you think this is true?

3. What are some ways people use color as camouflage or as a sign of danger?

Understanding cause and effect

A **cause** is the action that makes something happen. An **effect** is what happens as a result. In a sentence, the cause can come before the effect or after it.

Connecting words like *so* and *because* show a cause or an effect. Listen for them carefully. *So* shows an effect. *Because* shows a cause.

Pollution was a poison to the frogs, **so** the frogs in the pond died.

cause   effect

The frogs survived **because** their camouflage matched the leaves.

effect   cause

A. IDENTIFY Read and listen to these statements about the nature program you heard in Listening 1. Circle the cause in each statement. Underline the effect.

1. Katydids are hard to see because of their green color.

2. Predators can't see the katydids, so the katydids stay safe.

3. It's hard to see the cryptic frog because it uses camouflage.

4. The cryptic frog is the same color as the leaves, so you can't see it very well.

5. The blue poison dart frog is bright blue, so you can see it easily.

6. Dart frogs are dangerous because their skins contain a strong poison.

B. ANALYZE Listen to the scientist talk about Australian bowerbirds. Then match each cause with the correct effect.

A male bowerbird and its bower

Cause	Effect
____ 1. The satin bowerbird decorates its bower with blue things.	a. The bower looks nice.
____ 2. The bowerbird doesn't like red.	b. Predators cannot find the nest easily.
____ 3. The female builds a nest in a tree.	c. The bowerbird removes the red thing.

iQ PRACTICE Go online for more practice with listening to understand cause and effect. *Practice > Unit 2 > Activity 6*

CRITICAL THINKING STRATEGY

Evaluating cause-and-effect statements

A cause-and-effect statement makes a connection between two ideas. It says that one thing **caused** the other, which is the **effect**, or result. It is important to think critically about a statement like this. Ask, "Is it true, or valid?" A valid cause-and-effect statement is based on facts or something that is true.

Here is an example of a valid cause-and-effect statement.

It's dangerous to touch dart frogs because their skin contains a strong poison.

The statement is supported by the fact that scientists have proven that dart frogs are too poisonous even to touch. The cause is the poison, and the effect is that it's dangerous for people to touch dart frogs.

Here is a clearly false cause-and-effect statement.

It rained today because I washed my car. Every time I wash my car it rains.

There is no real connection between the rain and someone washing his or her car. The fact that two things often occur at the same time does not necessarily mean that one causes the other. There is no valid evidence to support this cause-and-effect statement.

iQ PRACTICE Go online to watch the Critical Thinking Video and check your comprehension. *Practice > Unit 2 > Activity 7*

C. **ANALYZE** Read these statements and decide if they show valid cause-and-effect relationships. Mark each one as *V* (valid) or *N* (not valid). Then write a sentence to explain your answer. Discuss your answers as a class.

1. The frog population declined this summer because there was no rain and it was very hot.

   V—This is probably valid because frogs need water to survive.

2. People say that katydids stop singing when it rains. Yesterday, it rained because the katydids stopped singing.

   _____

3. The bark of trees protects them from insects and weather. That tree died because someone cut all of the bark off it.

   _____

4. The bowerbird removed the stone from his bower because it was red, not blue. We see this again and again. He only puts blue things in his bower.

   _____

5. I just learned that bowerbirds exist, so they must be a newly discovered kind of bird.

   _____

Colorful Homes

You are going to listen to a class presentation about two different areas of the world where people enjoy very colorful houses. The presentation includes photographs of the houses. As you listen, gather information and ideas about how colors can be useful.

PREVIEW THE LISTENING

VOCABULARY SKILL REVIEW

In Unit 1, you learned about verb + noun collocations. Look for three or more verb + noun collocations in Activity A and underline them.

A. VOCABULARY Here are some words and phrases from Listening 2. Read the sentences. Then choose the sentence that best matches the meaning of the original sentence.

1. We painted the wall a <u>solid</u> red.

   a. The wall has only one color, red.

   b. The wall has a mix of red and other colors.

2. The flowers in the vase are a <u>brilliant</u> yellow.

   a. The flowers are dark yellow.

   b. The flowers are a very bright yellow.

3. The brown and red colors of the houses <u>blend in</u> with the desert landscape.

   a. The colors of the houses are similar to the colors of the desert.

   b. The colors of the houses are different from the colors of the desert.

4. It is difficult to draw a <u>straight</u> line if you don't have a ruler.

   a. It is hard to draw a line that goes directly from one point to another.

   b. It is hard to draw a perfect circle.

5. The garden is a very <u>peaceful</u> place to sit and relax.

   a. The garden is a noisy place with a lot of activity.

   b. The garden is a very calm and quiet place.

6. The design of the house is based on the <u>shape</u> of a triangle.

   a. The house has the same form as a triangle.

   b. The builder used a tool called a triangle to build the house.

7. The beauty and color of their homes give the women of Asir a sense of <u>pride</u>.

   a. They feel pleased and satisfied with their work.

   b. They can charge a lot for their work because it is good.

8. Look at those white clouds in the bright blue sky. They're really <u>beautiful</u>.

   a. It's probably going to rain soon.

   b. The sky and clouds are very nice to look at.

9. Look, the color of your scarf <u>matches</u> the color of my sweater.

   a. Your scarf and my sweater are the same color.

   b. The color of your scarf is more beautiful than the color of my sweater.

iQ PRACTICE   Go online for more practice with the vocabulary.
Practice > Unit 2 > Activities 8–9

B. PREVIEW Look at the two photos from the presentation. How are the colors different? Discuss with a partner.

A Luis Barragán building

A home in Asir, Saudi Arabia

WORK WITH THE LISTENING

🔊 **A. LISTEN AND TAKE NOTES** Listen to Part 1 of the panel presentation about the work of the Mexican architect Luis Barragán. Take notes. Remember to write only the most important words.

🔊 **B. LISTEN AND TAKE NOTES** Listen to Part 2 of the panel presentation about the houses in the province of Asir in Saudi Arabia. Take notes. Remember to write only the most important words.

🔊 **C. APPLY** Complete the summary of the presentations with the words and phrases in the box. Use your notes to help you. Then listen and check your answers.

Part 1:

architecture	bright colors	gardens	peaceful

The presentation was about the use of color in _____architecture_____ in
1

two different parts of the world, Mexico and the province of Asir in Saudi

Arabia. In Mexico, the architect Luis Barragán was famous for his use of

_____ in his buildings. The _____ around the
2 **3**

homes were also important to him. He wanted the homes he built to be beautiful

and _____ places for the people who lived there.
4

Part 2:

artistic	colorful designs	shapes	special tradition	women

The province of Asir in Saudi Arabia has a _____
5

of painting houses with _____ during the festival of Eid.
6

The designs use _____ like triangles and squares in many
7

different colors. The _____ do the painting, and they get a sense
8

of pride from making their homes beautiful. Today people are working to keep

this _____ tradition alive.
9

D. CATEGORIZE Work with a partner. Complete the chart with information about the two topics in the presentation. Then listen again and check your answers.

	Luis Barragán	The women of Asir
Country		
Typical colors		
Special features		

E. IDENTIFY Choose the answer that best completes each statement.

1. Luis Barragán used the colors of ____ in his architecture.

   a. buildings of American small towns

   b. houses in the small towns of Mexico

   c. houses in Mexico City

2. Barragán often painted the walls of his houses ____.

   a. with pictures of brightly colored flowers

   b. with complicated designs

   c. with strong, solid colors

3. Barragán liked the architecture of North Africa because ____.

   a. the houses were painted in bright colors

   b. the buildings blended in with the colors of the desert landscape

   c. the houses were large enough for many people to live in them

4. In the province of Asir, it is a tradition for people to paint their homes ____.

   a. every year

   b. every other year

   c. every five years

5. In the designs, lines going up and down are used to represent ____.

   a. houses

   b. water or lightning

   c. children

6. Competitions encourage modern artists ____.

   a. to create completely new designs for painting the houses

   b. to sell their artwork at fairs

   c. to use traditional designs in their artwork

F. CATEGORIZE Write *T* (true) or *F* (false). Then correct the false statements.

_____ 1. For Luis Barragán, the landscape and gardens around a house were not important.

_____

_____ 2. Barragán's travels to Europe and North Africa in the 1920s and 1930s had an influence on his architecture.

_____

_____ 3. The large triangles in the designs painted on the houses in Asir represent rivers near the home.

_____

_____ 4. The moderator of the panel discussion comments that the architectural traditions of Mexico and Saudi Arabia are similar in some ways.

_____

G. DISCUSS Work in a group. Look at the photos of the two living rooms. Which one would you prefer to have in your home? Why?

WORK WITH THE VIDEO

A. PREVIEW Why do you think color might be an important part of a company or product's image?

VIDEO VOCABULARY

image (n.) the general impression that a person, an organization, a product, etc., gives to the public

update (v.) to make something more modern

consistent (adj.) not changing

faded (adj.) lighter or less strong in color than the original

shade (n.) a type of a particular color, e.g., *a shade of green*

corporately (adv.) relating to a large business or a company

trustworthy (adj.) that you can trust, believe in, or depend on

iQ RESOURCES Go online to watch the video about how companies use color.
Resources > Video > Unit 2 > Unit Video

B. IDENTIFY Watch the video two or three times. While you watch, note which colors are mentioned. Match the colors with the items.

____ 1. UPS   a. yellow

____ 2. Home Depot   b. blue

____ 3. Something trustworthy   c. brown

____ 4. H&R Block   d. green

____ 5. traffic stoplight   e. orange

____ 6. New York City taxicabs   f. red

C. EXPLAIN Watch the video again. Work with a partner to ask and answer the questions.

1. Why is it important for a company's defining color to be consistent?

2. Why do most people think that blue stands for something that is dependable?

3. Why did H&R Block change their color?

4. What did people say about H&R Block's new color?

5. What examples does the video give of everyday things that will probably NOT change?

SAY WHAT YOU THINK

SYNTHESIZE Think about the unit video, Listening 1, and Listening 2 as you discuss the questions.

1. How can you compare the way animals use color with the way people use color?

2. Do any companies and businesses in your community use color branding? If so, what colors do they use? Are there any colors that would NOT be good for a company? Explain.

VOCABULARY SKILL **Word families: nouns and verbs**

Some words can be used as a **noun** or a **verb**. To know if a word is a noun or a verb, you have to look at the words around it.

There are pictures of the architect's **work** on the Internet. (noun)
The men **work** at the building site every day. (verb)

A word is probably a noun if it comes after . . .

- an article (*a, an,* or *the*).

- an adjective.

- a number.

- the words *this, that, these,* or *those*.

A word may be a verb if it comes after . . .

- a pronoun such as *it* or *they*.

- a time word such as *sometimes* or *never*.

- a helping verb such as *do, does, can, will,* or *should*.

A. CATEGORIZE Look at the bold word in each sentence. Write *N* (noun) or *V* (verb).

__V__ 1. We can **camouflage** this birdhouse. We can paint it the same color as the tree.

____ 2. An owl is a bird that flies at night. It calls, "Hoo, hoo, hoo." It **sounds** like it's asking, "Who? Who? Who?"

____ 3. The **poison** of that insect is very strong, but it can't kill a person.

____ 4. There are many different **sounds** in the forest at night.

____ 5. The colors of the insect's wings **blend in** with the leaves.

____ 6. Both of these shirts are blue, but the colors don't **match**. This one is darker.

____ 7. The color green is actually a **blend** of blue and yellow.

____ 8. That liquid is dangerous. It can **poison** people and animals.

The verb *change* is common in spoken and written academic English. It is often used with the prepositions *from* and *to*. *In winter, the color of the Arctic fox **changes from** brown **to** white.*

───────────────| **OPAL**
Oxford Phrasal Academic Lexicon

B. APPLY Complete each sentence with the correct word from the box. Then write *N* (noun) or *V* (verb).

camouflage	~~change~~	fight	match	poison	sound

1. When these birds are young, they are brown and white. When they become adults, their colors _____*change*_____ to black and orange.   V

2. When catbirds sing, the _____ is like cats meowing.   ____

3. Bowerbirds sometimes _____ other birds for building materials.   ____

4. They're trying to _____ the buildings by painting them brown and green.   ____

5. Can the skin of the dart frog _____ me if I touch it?   ____

6. Is the red in these shoes a good _____ with the red in my jacket?   ____

iQ PRACTICE Go online for more practice using word families.
Practice › Unit 2 › Activity 10

SPEAKING

OBJECTIVE ▶

At the end of this unit, you are going to design a house or an apartment building. Make sure to give examples when you describe the building to group members.

GRAMMAR *There's* and *it's*

There's (There is) is used when something is being mentioned for the first time.

- **There's** a <u>bookstore</u> on campus.
- **There's** a <u>software program</u> called Camouflage. It hides your files so others can't find them.
- **There's** a <u>tree</u> on the roof of that building!

The pronoun *it* in the expression *it's* (*it is*) refers to something we already know.

- The <u>dart frog</u> is bright blue. Predators know that **it's** dangerous.
- I don't like the <u>color</u> of that wall. **It's** too bright.

iQ RESOURCES Go online to watch the Grammar Skill Video.
Resources > Video > Unit 2 > Grammar Skill Video

A. APPLY Complete the paragraph with *there's* and *it's*.

TIP FOR SUCCESS

The pronoun *it* refers to both male and female animals. You can also use the pronouns *he* and *she* for animals when you know the gender of the animal.

There are many different animals in the park. _____There's_____ a
                                                        1
bright red bird in a tree. _____ a male cardinal. Nearby
                                    2
_____ a similar bird, but _____ brown, not red.
          3   4
_____ a female cardinal. On a flower, _____ a
          5   6
beautiful orange and black butterfly. _____ a monarch butterfly.
                                              7
Predators can see it easily. But they also know that _____
                                                              8
a dangerous insect. Its wings have a terrible taste. Its color is a warning to

predators.

B. COMPOSE Work with a partner. Imagine that you are in a place in your city. Describe what you see, using *there's* and *it's*. Take turns.

A: *There's a little store on that corner. I think it's a shoe store.*
B: *There's a new exhibition at the museum. It's about the first trip to the moon.*

iQ PRACTICE Go online for more practice with *there's* and *it's*.
Practice > Unit 2 > Activities 11–12

The **schwa** sound is the most common vowel sound in English. It is the same sound speakers make when they pause and say *Uh*. It is a very relaxed sound. Unstressed syllables often use the schwa. In dictionaries the pronunciation of the schwa is usually shown with the symbol /ə/.

The word *banana* is a good example of the schwa. The first and last syllables have the schwa. Note that the stressed syllable /næ/ is longer than the other syllables.

/bə ˈnæ nə/

The underlined syllables in these words also use the schwa. These are all unstressed syllables. Remember that any vowel can have the schwa sound.

a-<u>ni</u>-mal   poi-<u>son</u>   <u>sur</u>-vive   pre-<u>da</u>-<u>tor</u>   for-<u>est</u>

The schwa is common in unstressed syllables, but it is sometimes used in stressed syllables.

<u>hun</u>-gry   <u>mo</u>-ney

A. APPLY Listen and write the words. There is one unstressed syllable with the schwa sound in each word. Circle the syllable that contains the schwa sound.

1. ca<u>mou</u>flage
2. _____
3. _____
4. _____

5. _____
6. _____
7. _____
8. _____

B. IDENTIFY Listen again. Then practice with a partner. Take turns saying the words.

C. EVALUATE Listen to these pairs of words. Which word has the schwa sound in the underlined syllable? Circle your answers.

1. <u>tra</u>dition   <u>traf</u>fic
2. <u>men</u>tion   ele<u>ment</u>
3. <u>an</u>swer   a<u>no</u>ther
4. <u>pro</u>gram   <u>pro</u>tection

D. APPLY Work with a partner. Underline all the syllables with the schwa sound. Then take turns reading the sentences.

1. It is a traditional festival that we celebrate every year.

2. Is there an apartment for rent on State Street?

3. We need to find another answer to the problem.

4. There's a special program to protect the city's water.

iQ PRACTICE Go online for more practice with schwa in unstressed syllables.
Practice > Unit 2 > Activity 13

SPEAKING SKILL Asking for and giving examples

When you explain something, give **examples** to help the listener understand your ideas. When you don't understand something a speaker says, ask for an example.

Giving an example:

⌈ For example, . . .
  For instance, . . .
⌊ Here's an example.

Asking for an example:

⌈ Can you give me an example?
⌊ Do you have any examples?

A. ANALYZE Listen to the excerpts from the Listenings in this unit. How do the speakers introduce or ask for examples? Write the expressions they use.

1. _____

2. _____

3. _____

4. _____

B. PRACTICE Work with a partner. Choose one of the topics below. Tell your partner about the topic. Take turns asking for and giving examples.

- the best colors for the rooms of a house

- why I love the colors of the desert (or the mountains, the beach, etc.)

- my favorite colors to wear

iQ PRACTICE Go online for more practice with asking for and giving examples.
Practice > Unit 2 > Activity 14

UNIT ASSIGNMENT Present a building design

OBJECTIVE ▶

In this section, you are going to present a design of a house or an apartment building. As you prepare your design, think about the Unit Question, "How can colors be useful?" Use information from Listening 1, Listening 2, the unit video, and your work in this unit to support your presentation. Refer to the Self-Assessment checklist on page 45.

CONSIDER THE IDEAS

DISCUSS Look at the photos. Then discuss the questions in a group.

1. Which building do you like the most? Why?

2. Which building do you like the least? Why?

3. Do you like buildings that blend into their environments or buildings that are unusual? Explain.

PREPARE AND SPEAK

A. GATHER IDEAS Work in a group. You are going to design a building. Complete the steps.

1. Decide on the type of building. Is it an apartment building or a house?

2. Choose a location for the building. Is your building in a city, a town, or the country? _____ Our building is in a ____.

   a. desert area: dry without many green plants

   b. forest area: green with a lot of trees

   c. large city: downtown with a lot of people and buildings

   d. large city: quiet street near the edge of the city

   e. beach town: near the ocean

B. ORGANIZE IDEAS Discuss with your group what the building looks like from the outside. Then create an outline, using the categories below. Use visual elements in your notes to help show what your building looks like.

- building type
- location
- materials (concrete, wood, glass, metal, etc.)
- outside colors
- plan (how big, how many floors, how many rooms, etc.)
- blends in or is unusual?

C. SPEAK Present your building design to another group. Refer to the Self-Assessment checklist on page 45 before you begin.

1. Use your outline and visual elements from Activity B to help you.

2. Make sure that each person in the group takes part in the presentation.

3. Give examples and show some visual elements to help your audience to better understand.

iQ PRACTICE Go online for your alternate Unit Assignment.
Practice > Unit 2 > Activity 15

CHECK AND REFLECT

A. CHECK Think about the Unit Assignment as you complete the Self-Assessment checklist.

SELF-ASSESSMENT	Yes	No
I used visual elements to show my ideas.	☐	☐
I was able to speak easily about the topic.	☐	☐
My audience understood me.	☐	☐
I used *there's* and *it's*.	☐	☐
I used vocabulary from the unit.	☐	☐
I asked for and gave examples.	☐	☐
I used the schwa in unstressed syllables.	☐	☐

B. REFLECT Discuss these questions with a partner or group.

1. What is something new you learned in this unit?

2. Look back at the Unit Question—How can colors be useful? Is your answer different now than when you started this unit? If yes, how is it different? Why?

iQ PRACTICE Go to the online discussion board to discuss the questions. *Practice > Unit 2 > Activity 16*

TRACK YOUR SUCCESS

iQ PRACTICE Go online to check the words and phrases you have learned in this unit. *Practice > Unit 2 > Activity 17*

Check (✓) the skills you learned. If you need more work on a skill, refer to the page(s) in parentheses.

NOTE-TAKING	☐ I can use visual elements. (p. 26)
LISTENING	☐ I can understand cause and effect. (p. 31)
CRITICAL THINKING	☐ I can evaluate cause-and-effect statements. (p. 32)
VOCABULARY	☐ I can use noun and verb word families. (p. 39)
GRAMMAR	☐ I can use *there's* and *it's*. (p. 41)
PRONUNCIATION	☐ I can use the schwa in unstressed syllables. (p. 42)
SPEAKING	☐ I can ask for and give examples. (p. 43)
OBJECTIVE ▶	☐ I can gather information and ideas to participate in a group presentation about the uses of color.

Why are social skills important?

A. Discuss these questions with your classmates.

1. What are social skills? Give examples. *say Thanx excuseme*

2. Are you ever unsure about what to do in social situations? Give examples.

3. Look at the photo. What are some things we do to make social situations easier? *sift to help people*

🔊 **B.** Listen to *The Q Classroom* online. Then answer these questions.

1. What does Yuna say about social skills?

2. What ideas do Sophy and Felix add to Yuna's? *to buil relatioship*

3. What kind of course did Marcus take?

iQ PRACTICE Go to the online discussion board to discuss the Unit Question with your classmates. *Practice > Unit 3 > Activity 1*

UNIT OBJECTIVE ▶ Listen to a radio program and a news report. Gather information and ideas to give a presentation about manners.

LISTENING 1

OBJECTIVE ▶

Be Polite

You are going to listen to a radio program called *Book Talk*. The people on the program talk about the book *The Civility Solution: What to Do When People Are Rude* by P. M. Forni. It is about the need for more polite behavior in our society. As you listen, gather information and ideas about why social skills are important.

PREVIEW THE LISTENING

ACADEMIC LANGUAGE

The word *behavior* is commonly used when speaking in academic English. The adjectives *good, bad, polite*, and *rude* are often used to describe behavior. *No one likes his rude behavior.*

_____ | OPAL
Oxford Phrasal Academic Lexicon

A. VOCABULARY Here are some words from Listening 1. Read the definitions. Then circle the best word to complete each sentence.

> **behavior** (noun) ⚷ OPAL the way you act
> **courtesy** (noun) pleasant behavior that shows respect for other people
> *(E-ti-ket)*
> **etiquette** (noun) the rules for courtesy and polite behavior
> **manners** (noun) ⚷ acceptable behavior in a culture
> **polite** (adjective) ⚷ having good manners and showing courtesy
> **rude** (adjective) ⚷ not polite

⚷ Oxford 3000™ words OPAL Oxford Phrasal Academic Lexicon

1. You should always treat coworkers with (behavior /(courtesy)) and respect. Good manners are important at work.

2. Miteb's ((behavior)/ courtesy) in today's class was terrible. He arrived late, he talked on his cell phone, and then he went to sleep!

Handwritten annotations: "Polite < courteous", "How you treat others", "basic in work", "How you behave"

3. I'm nervous about dining in the restaurant tonight. There are so many different glasses and forks on the table. Can I borrow your book about (etiquette / behavior)?

4. When you stay at a friend's house, it is (polite / rude) to write him or her a thank-you note. It shows you are a good friend.

5. That child was very rude to everyone. Parents should teach their kids better (manners / courtesy).

VOCABULARY SKILL REVIEW

In Unit 2, you learned that some words can be used as a noun or a verb. Circle the underlined words in Activity B that can be used as both a noun and a verb.

B. IDENTIFY Read the sentences. Then choose the answer that best matches the meaning of each underlined word.

1. I admit that I made a mistake. I was rude to Sara.

   a. agree it is true

   b. think it is wrong

2. Different cultures and groups of people have different ideas about what's OK. In that society, it's normal for people to arrive late.

   a. a group of people at a school

   b. the people of one country or area

3. There have been more accidents lately. One reason for the increase in car accidents is that people don't pay attention to the road.

   a. smaller number

   b. growing number

4. There's too much violence in video games. It's not good to see characters fight and kill.

   a. rude or impolite words

   b. actions done to hurt someone

5. When a soccer player scores a goal, the people in the stadium often scream with excitement. The noise is incredible!

   a. speak in very loud voices

   b. speak very quietly

iQ PRACTICE Go online for more practice with the vocabulary.
Practice > Unit 3 > Activities 2–3

LISTENING SKILL Predicting

As a listener, you can't always **predict**, or guess, what you are going to hear. There's no way to know what people are going to talk about at an event or what you are going to hear on the street. At other times, you can predict the topic—for example, in a class, on TV, or on the radio. In these cases, you can prepare to listen.

- Find out about the topic. For a radio or TV program, look at the program guide. For a class, check the class schedule or your notes from the last class.

- Ask, "What do I know about this topic?"

For example, if you are going to watch a TV documentary about tigers, you might ask questions like these.

What do I know about tigers?
What do they look like?
Where do they live?

Road rage

Bad no

C. PREVIEW You are going to listen to people on a radio program talk about the need for more polite behavior in our society. What do you think is the best way to respond to a rude person? Discuss your idea with a partner.

D. DISCUSS Listen to three parts of the radio program. Before you listen to each part, discuss the question with a partner. Predict what the speaker will say. Listen to check your prediction.

Part 1 The host of the program is going to introduce his guest. What information do you think he will include? *budder than post*

Part 2 What question did the host ask at the end of Part 1? How do you think Lynn Hancock will answer this question?

Part 3 How does the host feel about being polite when others are rude? What will Hancock say about this? *Rude = 作らない失礼* *Rude = Rude* *fight* *Don't X Rude*

iQ PRACTICE Go online for more practice with predicting.
Practice > Unit 3 > Activity 4

iQ PRACTICE Go online for additional listening and comprehension.
Practice > Unit 3 > Activity 5

Civil = The man behaved in a civil manner by not shouting at me
(adj)

WORK WITH THE LISTENING

A. LISTEN AND TAKE NOTES Listen to the program again. As you listen, think about these key words and phrases. Why is each one important? Use the words in your notes.

bad manners	polite	the "civility solution"	road rage
increase	rudeness	journalist	violence

B. CATEGORIZE Read the statements. Write *T* (true) or *F* (false). Use your notes to help you.

__F__ 1. Professor Forni says people are more polite now than in the past.

__T__ 2. Professor Forni says rudeness can cause social problems.

__F__ 3. Professor Forni says there is no connection between rudeness and stress.

__T__ 4. The best idea is to be polite when people are rude to you.

__T__ 5. It's OK to say that you don't like someone's behavior.

TIP FOR SUCCESS

As you listen, try to think ahead. Ask, "What's next? What is the speaker going to say?"

C. IDENTIFY Read the sentences. Choose the answer that best completes each statement. Then listen and check your answers.

1. The host of the program is ____.

   a. Scott Webber

   b. John Hopkins

   c. Lynn Hancock

2. "Road rage" is a term used to describe drivers who ____.

   a. get angry while driving

   b. are not good drivers

   c. drive too fast

3. If someone is yelling at you, you should ____.

   a. scream at them

   b. say nothing and walk away

   c. stay calm and speak politely

4. Lynn tells a story about something that happened to her when she was ____.

   a. driving her car

   b. riding on a bus

   c. riding on the subway

D. EXPLAIN Lynn Hancock tells a story to show how the "civility solution" worked for her. Work with a partner. Take turns asking and answering the questions.

1. What happened?

2. Was it an accident or did she do it on purpose?

3. What did the man do?

4. How did Lynn respond?

5. Was the "civility solution" successful in this case?

E. IDENTIFY Work in a group. Read the excerpt from Listening 1 and fill in the missing words. Then listen and check your answers.

Well, that's where the "civility _____" comes in. When someone
                                    1

is _____ to us, it's natural, or _____,
              2   3

to be rude to them. You're rude to me, so I'm rude to you. It's a

_____ of rudeness. But, when we're _____
              4   5

to someone who is rude, it _____ the circle. In other
                                          6

_____, you're rude to me, but I'm polite to you. If people can
              7

learn to do this, our _____ will be better.
                              8

CRITICAL THINKING STRATEGY

Applying what you learn

Sometimes understanding what you hear—for example, in a lecture or a conversation—is not enough. You may need to apply what you learn to real-life situations. For example, in a math class, you learn skills you may need for your job or solving problems around your home. In a history class, you learn about events from the past. Then you can compare these with events today and think about what we can learn from the past.

In the following activities, you will explore how you might apply Professor Forni's ideas and your learning to new situations.

iQ PRACTICE   Go online to watch the Critical Thinking Video and check your comprehension. *Practice > Unit 3 > Activity 6*

F. **CREATE** Work with a partner. Choose one of these situations. Create a conversation to practice the civility solution. One person will be A and the other will be B. Use these examples to get you started.

Situation 1: A meeting of coworkers in an office to discuss ways to make the office a better place to work.

A: Suggest that workers collect money to buy a coffee machine for the office.

A: *We really need a new coffee machine for the office. If we all give five dollars, we can buy one.*

B: Say that A's idea is "ridiculous."

A: Respond to B. Use the civility solution.

Situation 2: Two people sitting next to each other on a train. There's a sign above the seats that says "As a courtesy to other passengers, please do not use your cell phone on the train."

A: You are talking loudly to a friend on your cell phone.

A: *Hi, you know we had a great time yesterday at . . .*

B: Ask A politely to stop talking on the cell phone. Point to the sign.

A: Tell B that you will stop "in a minute," but keep on talking.

B: Ask A to stop talking on the cell phone. Be polite, but firm. Use the civility solution.

G. **DISCUSS** Act out your conversation for the class. How are your classmates' conversations similar to or different from yours? Discuss as a class.

SAY WHAT YOU THINK

DISCUSS Discuss the questions in a small group.

1. Think of a time when someone was rude to you. What did you do and say?

2. What do you think of Professor Forni's ideas? Are they easy to follow? Do they work? Why or why not?

3. Imagine that many people start to follow Professor Forni's ideas. Can this change society?

When you take notes, it is important to organize the notes on the page. First, write the topic at the top of the page. Do this before the class begins if you can. When the class begins, make a quick outline for your notes. For example, an instructor might say something like, "Today we're going to talk about three ways in which rudeness hurts individuals and our society." This tells you that there are three main points to listen for. If this happens, write the numbers 1, 2, 3 on the page. Leave space after each number to write notes.

Read the introduction to a presentation about the use of color in architecture. Notice that the student wrote a few key words about the topic at the top of the page. The student then prepared space for the two main topics in the discussion and copied the names the instructor wrote on the board.

> Today we're going to discuss the work of two architects and their use of color. First, you will see some examples of the work of the Mexican architect Luis Barragán. Then we'll move on to the work of young French architect Emmanuelle Moureaux. Moureaux's use of happy colors in her work makes some refer to her as a "Joymaker."

architecture, use of color

1. Luis Barragán

2. Emmanuelle Moureaux

 A. APPLY Listen to the introduction to a talk titled "A History of Rude Behavior." Then prepare a page you could use to take notes.

B. EXTEND Compare your note page with a partner. Answer the questions.

1. How many topics did the speaker mention?

2. How did you describe each topic?

iQ PRACTICE Go online for more practice with organizing notes.
Practice › Unit 3 › Activity 7

Classroom Etiquette

OBJECTIVE ▶

You are going to listen to a news report about teaching etiquette in the classroom. Teachers think that students need to learn better manners. The question is, "Who should teach manners, parents or teachers?" As you listen, gather information and ideas about why social skills are important.

Polite ← (courteous (adj)) (adj)

PREVIEW THE LISTENING

A. VOCABULARY Here are some words and phrases from Listening 2. Read the definitions. Then complete each sentence with the correct word or phrase.

Higher manner than polite

---

attentive *(adjective)* watching or listening carefully

courteous *(adjective)* polite, having courtesy

deal with *(verb phrase)* to solve a problem

improve *(verb)* ꙮ OPAL to make something better

influence *(noun)* ꙮ OPAL the power to change how someone or something acts

principal *(noun)* the person in charge of a school

respect *(noun)* ꙮ OPAL consideration for the rights and feelings of other people

shout out *(verb phrase)* to say something in a loud voice

valuable *(adjective)* ꙮ OPAL very useful or important

ꙮ Oxford 3000™ words   **OPAL** Oxford Phrasal Academic Lexicon

✓ 1. I apologized to show Sue I have ____respect____ for her feelings.

✓ 2. The parents are meeting with the ____principal____ tonight to discuss problems at school. She can make new school rules to stop the problems.

3. Parents can have a great ____influence____ on a child's behavior. They can teach by setting an example.

4. Teachers have to ___deal with___ many difficult problems in the classroom every day. They think of many good solutions.

5. Everyone thought that the class was very ___valuable___. It helped them get better grades and it improved their social skills.

6. I don't like it when people in a meeting just ___shout out___ their comments. They should wait their turn and speak politely.

7. Lisa and Mark want to ___Improve___ their Spanish. They go to class every day and practice often.

8. Young children can only be ___attentive___ for 20 or 30 minutes at a time. It is hard for them to sit still and focus for a long time.

9. Your son is very ___courteoust___ at school. He calls me Ms. Moore, and he always says *please* and *thank you*.

iQ PRACTICE Go online for more practice with the vocabulary.
Practice > Unit 3 > Activities 8–9

B. PREVIEW You are going to listen to a news report about teaching etiquette in the classroom. What do you think parents and teachers say about the etiquette classes? Choose *a* or *b*. Then explain your choice to a partner.

a. They like the classes. They feel they have a positive effect on the children's behavior.

b. The classes are a waste of time. Kids have to learn good manners at home.

WORK WITH THE LISTENING

A. LISTEN AND TAKE NOTES Prepare a page for note-taking. Write a few key words and a short outline. Then listen to the first part of the news report about teaching etiquette in the classroom.

B. APPLY Listen to the rest of the news report and take notes. Use the page you prepared in Activity A.

C. APPLY Read the sentences. Choose the answer that best completes each statement. Use your notes to help you.

1. The main point of the news report is that ___c___. *a*

   a. parents don't know how to teach their children good manners

   b. teachers don't have time to teach manners in the classroom

   c. some schools teach manners in the classroom

(adj.)
Punctual
" on time

The student was very Punctual, he always came to the class on time.

2. According to Marjorie Lucas, the most important idea about manners is that __a__. _c_

   a. children need to respect other people

   b. fighting and violence are bad

   c. children need to have good table manners

3. The report makes it clear that __c__. _c_

   a. parents are better than schools at teaching manners

   b. the results of the etiquette classes surprised teachers

   c. the etiquette classes helped children, teachers, and parents

🔊 **D. IDENTIFY** Work with a partner. Try to find information in your notes about each of these items. Listen again and add to your notes, if necessary.

1. one example of polite behavior for children around adults — _use Mr. Mrs._

2. the name of the company that teaches etiquette classes — _Polit Firm_

3. one example of good behavior at school — _use excu me Pahk_   _raise hands_   _30%_

4. two positive results from the etiquette classes _grade went up 10 — 30% / less violence_

5. how parents feel about the etiquette classes _like the class_
   They are suprised

🔊 **E. EVALUATE** Listen to four sentences from the news report. Choose the sentence that is closest in meaning to the one you hear.

1. _b_ (a.) When teachers have to spend time dealing with bad behavior, they have less time to teach other things.

   b. For teachers, dealing with bad behavior is the most important part of their job.

2. _b_ (a.) When children do small things, like saying "please" and "thank you," it shows that they have respect for others.

   b. Children can be courteous in small ways, but that doesn't mean they respect other people.

3. a. Students earned good grades in the etiquette classes during the school year.

   _b_ (b.) Because of the etiquette classes, students got better grades in their classwork.

4. _a_ (a.) Students listen more carefully when they are in class.

   b. Students aren't absent from class as much as they were in the past.

F. **CREATE** Look at the list of rules that a teacher made for the classroom. Complete each sentence on the list with a phrase from the box. Then add one more "rule" to the list. Use your own idea.

get into fights	shout out the answer	say "Excuse me"
raise your hand	Mr., Ms., or Mrs.	say "Thank you"
say "Please"		

CLASSROOM RULES

1. When you want to answer a question, _raise your hand_.

2. Don't _shout out the answer_ when I ask a question.

3. When you speak to teachers or to the principal, use _Mr, Ms or Mrs_ and their last name.

4. If you bump into someone, _Say Excuse me_.

5. When you ask for something, _Pleas_.

6. Don't _get into fights_ in the hallway or on the playground.

7. When someone gives you something, _____.

8. _Thank you_

WORK WITH THE VIDEO

talk with stranger
· speak not deep story
· talk weator

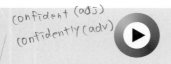

confident (adj)
confidently (adv)

A. PREVIEW Before you watch the video on making "small talk," discuss this question with a partner: How do you feel when you are in room with a lot of people you don't know?

VIDEO VOCABULARY

rapport (n.) a friendly situation in which people understand each other

initiate (v.) ɪnˈɪʃieɪt to start something

snippet (n.) a small piece of something

confidence (n.) trust or belief in someone or something

contentious debate (n.) angry argument

Handwritten notes at top:
tagline → give a litle bit into more
→ invite a question ~~more~~ saying my name
Hi I'm Yuta   than
I'm studying English

iQ RESOURCES Go online to watch the video about a class learning the social skill of making "small talk." *Resources > Video > Unit 3 > Unit Video*

B. CATEGORIZE Watch the video two or three times and take notes. Then read the statements. Write *T* (true) or *F* (false). Use your notes to help you.

(handwritten T) ~~X~~ 1. The expert says that "small talk" has that name because it isn't important.

(handwritten ✓) T 2. Small talk helps build rapport among people. *(handwritten: (statement)   connection)*

(handwritten F) ~~X~~ 3. A tag line is a type of question.

(handwritten ✓) F 4. A passive participant in a conversation asks questions.

(handwritten ✓) F 5. Small talk should include comments about your health problems.

(handwritten ✓) T 6. It's not OK to get into a big argument with someone you just met.

(handwritten ✓) T 7. People who are good at small talk enjoy conversations more.

(handwritten ✓) T 8. People who are good at small talk make better connections.

C. EXTEND Do you agree that the ability to make small talk is an important social skill? Why or why not? Discuss the questions in a small group. Give examples to support your opinion.

SAY WHAT YOU THINK

SYNTHESIZE Think about the unit video, Listening 1, and Listening 2 as you discuss the questions.

1. How did you learn about etiquette and social skills? Did you learn from your parents? Teachers? Other sources? Give examples.

2. What would Professor Forni think about companies giving etiquette classes in schools?

3. Marjorie Lucas, from the company Polite Children, said, "In the end, manners are all about having respect for others." How can you apply this idea in your daily life?

VOCABULARY SKILL Synonyms

Words with the same or very similar meanings are called **synonyms**. Synonyms can make your speaking and writing more interesting.

Dictionaries show the meanings of synonyms, and they provide helpful examples about how to use synonyms.

Dictionaries often give synonyms at the end of entries, and the example sentences at different entries show you how to use the words correctly. For example, look at these definitions of the words *anger* and *rage*. *Anger* and *rage* are synonyms, but *rage* is a stronger feeling than *anger*.

> **anger¹** /ˈæŋgər/ *noun* [U] the strong feeling that you have when something has happened or someone has done something that you do not like: *He could not hide his anger at the news.* ◆ *She was shaking with anger.*

> **rage¹** /reɪdʒ/ *noun* [C, U] a feeling of violent anger that is difficult to control: *He was trembling with rage.* ◆ *to fly into a rage*

All dictionary entries adapted from the *Oxford American Dictionary for learners of English* © Oxford University Press 2011.

A. APPLY Match each word on the left with a synonym on the right. Use your dictionary to help you.

manners (n),
say "Thank you"
say "Please"

✓ __c__ 1. courteous *adj*   a. growth (n)

✓ __b__ 2. rude   b. impolite

✓ __d__ 3. scream   c. polite

✓ __f__ 4. valuable *adj*   d. yell

✓ __e__ 5. etiquette *n*   e. manners

✓ __a__ 6. increase (v) (n)   f. important

B. RESTATE Synonyms work well in these sentences. Rewrite each sentence using a synonym for the word or words in bold.

money ✗ *no*

bill (s) *ok*

1. I think it's **rude** to use your cell phone on the bus.

   I think it's impolite to use your cell phone on the bus.

2. Please tell the kids outside to stop **screaming**. My students are taking a test.

   Please tell the kids outside to stop yelling .

3. If salespeople are **courteous**, they'll probably make more sales.

   If salespeople're polite , they'll

4. Emily Post wrote many books about **good manners**.

   Emily Post wrote many books about good etiquette .

iQ PRACTICE Go online for more practice with synonyms.
Practice > Unit 3 > Activity 10

SPEAKING

OBJECTIVE ▶

At the end of this unit, you are going to work in a group to give a presentation about using manners in a particular situation. As part of the presentation, you will have to give advice about what people should and should not do in the situation.

GRAMMAR Modal verbs *should* and *shouldn't*

Use **should** and **shouldn't** to give and ask for *advice* and *recommendations*.

Affirmative: You **should** be polite, even when someone is rude to you.
☐ You **should** wear a suit and tie to the interview.

Negative: We **shouldn't** let people say rude things to us.
☐ You **shouldn't** speak Spanish when Ron is here. He doesn't understand it.

Questions: **Should** our listeners read the book?
☐ What **should** we do about the kids who wrote on the wall at school?

---

iQ RESOURCES Go online to watch the Grammar Skill Video.
Resources > Video > Unit 3 > Grammar Skill Video

laugh at

A. APPLY Complete each sentence with *should* or *shouldn't*. Use your own opinions.

1. Your best friend thinks she is sending an email to her parents. She sends it to you by mistake. You ___shouldn't___ read it.

2. A woman ___should___ open the door for a man carrying a large box.

3. Children ___should___ call their teachers by their first names.

4. University students ___should___ raise their hands to ask a question in class.

5. You ___shouldn't___ call people after 10 p.m.

6. Men ___should___ stand up when a woman comes into the room.

7. You ___should___ tell someone if they have spinach in their teeth.

8. You're sitting on a crowded bus. An older woman gets on. You ___should___ offer her your seat.

B. EXPLAIN Work with a partner. Take turns asking and answering *Yes/No* questions based on the sentences in Activity A. Explain your answers.

A: *Should you read your friend's email to her parents?*
B: *No, you shouldn't. You should tell your friend about it.*

iQ PRACTICE Go online for more practice with the modal verbs *should* and *shouldn't*. *Practice* > *Unit 3* > *Activity 11*

iQ PRACTICE Go online for the Grammar Expansion: modal verbs *have to* and *has to*. *Practice* > *Unit 3* > *Activity 12*

PRONUNCIATION Final /s/ or /z/ sounds

Words ending in /s/ or /z/ sounds link, or connect, to words beginning with a vowel. Listen to these examples.

It's easy to make small talk.

The man was mad at the other drivers around him.

A. IDENTIFY Read the sentences. Mark the /s/ and /z/ sounds that link to vowels.

1. The students admitted they made a mistake.

2. Parents are too busy to teach their children manners.

3. The book talks about different ways to deal with problems.

4. Bad manners are a problem in our office.

5. I was amazed by my visit to the Great Wall.

6. Is it possible for them to deal with the problem today?

TIP FOR SUCCESS

Learning how to link words will make your speech sound more natural and fluent. It can also make it easier to pronounce final sounds clearly.

B. APPLY Work with a partner. Practice saying the sentences in Activity A. Listen and check your pronunciation.

C. EXTEND Listen to the paragraph about the etiquette of hats. Complete the paragraph with the words you hear. Then read the story to a partner.

Franklin D. Roosevelt, 1944

John F. Kennedy, 1963

THE ETIQUETTE OF HATS

There are a lot of _____ about _____ in etiquette books.
                           1   2

_____ _____, men and women always wore _____
         3   4   5

_____. It was bad _____ to go out without a hat. Men took off their
         6   7

_____ _____. It _____ _____ sign of
         8   9   10   11

respect for a man to take off his hat. These rules started to change in the 1960s. John F. Kennedy was

the first U.S. president to appear in public without a hat.

iQ PRACTICE Go online for more practice with final /s/ or /z/ sounds.
Practice ▸ Unit 3 ▸ Activity 13

SPEAKING SKILL Giving advice and making recommendations

When you give **advice** or make **recommendations**, you don't want the listener to think that you're giving commands. To make sure the listener understands, you can use expressions like these.

I think you should . . .
I don't think you should . . .
Don't you think you should . . . ?
Maybe you shouldn't . . .

A. CREATE Work with a partner. Read the sentences. Take turns giving advice.

1. **A:** It is hard to get to class on time. What should I do?

   B: I think you should . . .

2. **A:** My homework is very messy. It is difficult for the teacher to read.

   B: Don't you think you should . . . ?

3. **A:** Alan invited me to his house for dinner, but I don't know anybody there!

   B: Maybe you should/shouldn't . . .

4. **A:** My friends send me text messages when I'm in class. It's hard to pay attention in class when they send me messages.

   B: Well, I don't think you should . . .

B. EXTEND Work with a partner. Choose one of the topics below. Ask your partner for advice. Then give your partner advice about the problem he or she chooses.

1. You are going to a formal dinner at someone's home. Ask for advice about what to wear, what time to arrive, what to bring, what to talk about with guests, and table manners.

2. You are in charge of a committee. The committee's job is to improve your workplace or classroom. The goal is to encourage people to be more courteous to each other. Ask for advice about what the committee should do.

iQ PRACTICE   Go online for more practice with giving advice and making recommendations. *Practice > Unit 3 > Activity 14*

UNIT ASSIGNMENT   Give a presentation on manners

OBJECTIVE ▶

In this section, you are going to give a short presentation about manners. As you prepare your presentation, think about the Unit Question, "Why are social skills important?" Use information from Listening 1, Listening 2, the unit video, and your work in this unit to support your presentation. Refer to the Self-Assessment checklist on page 66.

CONSIDER THE IDEAS

EVALUATE Read the list of statements and check (✓) the ones you agree with.

☐ People don't always need to have good manners.

☐ I think people should learn proper etiquette.

☐ Manners should be taught at home, not at school.

☐ I prefer to be with people who have good manners.

☐ People should know how to behave at all times.

☐ Good table manners are not very important.

PREPARE AND SPEAK

A. GATHER IDEAS Work in a group. Choose one presentation topic from the box or think of your own topic.

Bad manners for . . .
• children at home
• driving a car
• eating with family or friends
• riding on a train or bus
• students in the classroom

B. ORGANIZE IDEAS Prepare a short presentation on the topic your group picked in Activity A. Use the outline to help you organize your ideas. Give at least two examples.

Topic: Bad manners for _____

1. What some people do: _____

   Why is this an example of bad manners?

   Reasons:

   a. _____

   b. _____

   What people should do: _____

   Reasons:

   a. _____

   b. _____

2. What some people do: _____

   Why is this an example of bad manners?

   Reasons:

   a. _____

   b. _____

   What people should do: _____

   Reasons:

   a. _____

   b. _____

C. SPEAK Present your ideas to the class or to another group. Refer to the Self-Assessment checklist below before you begin.

1. Make sure each member of your group presents at least one idea in the presentation. For example, one person can describe an example of bad manners.

2. In your presentation, explain:

   - why you chose the topic.
   - why the behaviors are bad.
   - examples of bad manners.
   - how people should behave.

iQ PRACTICE   Go online for your alternate Unit Assignment.
Practice > Unit 3 > Activity 15

CHECK AND REFLECT

A. CHECK Think about the Unit Assignment as you complete the Self-Assessment checklist.

SELF-ASSESSMENT	Yes	No
I was able to speak easily about the topic.	☐	☐
My group or class understood me.	☐	☐
I used *should* and *shouldn't*.	☐	☐
I used vocabulary from the unit.	☐	☐
I gave advice and I made recommendations.	☐	☐
I connected final /s/ and /z/ sounds to vowels.	☐	☐

B. REFLECT Discuss these questions with a partner or group.

1. What is something new you learned in this unit?

2. Look back at the Unit Question—Why are social skills important? Is your answer different now than when you started this unit? If yes, how is it different? Why?

iQ PRACTICE   Go to the online discussion board to discuss these questions.
Practice > Unit 3 > Activity 16

TRACK YOUR SUCCESS

iQ PRACTICE Go online to check the words and phrases you have learned in this unit. *Practice > Unit 3 > Activity 17*

Check (✓) the skills you learned. If you need more work on a skill, refer to the page(s) in parentheses.

LISTENING	☐ I can predict. (p. 50)
CRITICAL THINKING	☐ I can apply what I've learned. (p. 52)
NOTE-TAKING	☐ I can organize notes. (p. 54)
VOCABULARY	☐ I can use synonyms. (p. 60)
GRAMMAR	☐ I can use the modal verbs *should* and *shouldn't*. (p. 61)
PRONUNCIATION	☐ I can connect final /s/ or /z/ sounds. (p. 62)
SPEAKING	☐ I can give advice and make recommendations. (p. 63)

OBJECTIVE ▶ ☐ I can gather information and ideas to give a presentation about social skills.

Technology

4

NOTE-TAKING	using symbols and abbreviations
CRITICAL THINKING	curiosity
LISTENING	listening for specific information
VOCABULARY	using the dictionary
GRAMMAR	comparatives
PRONUNCIATION	linking between consonant sounds
SPEAKING	asking for and giving clarification

How does technology affect our relationships?

A. Discuss these questions with your classmates.

1. What kinds of electronic devices do you use every day? Examples include cell phones and GPS trackers.

2. About how many hours each day do you spend using these devices at work? At school? At home?

3. Look at the picture. When you're with your friends or family, do you spend more time talking or using an electronic device?

B. Listen to *The Q Classroom* online. Then match the ideas to the students.

____ 1. We still need face time with each other.   a. Felix

____ 2. It's easier to keep in touch with friends.   b. Sophy

____ 3. My friends and I don't talk like we used to.   c. Marcus

____ 4. We have one night a week as family night.   d. Yuna

iQ PRACTICE   Go to the online discussion board to discuss the Unit Question with your classmates. *Practice › Unit 4 › Activity 1*

UNIT OBJECTIVE ▶ Listen to a lecture and a conversation. Gather information and ideas to participate in a panel discussion about how technology affects our relationships.

NOTE-TAKING SKILL Using symbols and abbreviations

Many people now communicate by texting each other on their cell phones. To save time when they text, people use symbols and shortened forms of common words and expressions. Symbols and abbreviations are also useful for note-taking. The following list has some common symbols and abbreviations.

=	*equals, is the same as*	**w, w/o**	*with, without*
&	*and*	**etc.**	*and so on, and more*
e.g.	*for example*	**+**	*plus, more than*
re	*about*	**v.**	*very*

You can also create your own abbreviations. Abbreviate long words or frequently repeated words. Use initials for the names of people or organizations after the first use. Write numbers as numerals instead of words, e.g., 4 (not *four*). Just be sure that you can remember what your abbreviations stand for!

A. COMPOSE Read this student's notes about an inventor. Write a complete version of what you think the notes say. Then compare with a partner.

Alex. Graham Bell b. 1847 Scot. scientist

1870 moved to Canada, prov. of Ontario & set up workshop

1874 Ass't was Thomas Watson

1876 invent. 1st working tel. w/ TW's help

Mar. 10 '76 1st tel. call. AGB called TW (in next room)
   said "Mr. W. come here, I want you."

1877 AGB start Bell Tel. Co.

1886 150,000+ in US have tel. in home

 B. APPLY Listen to this short talk about the telegraph invented by Samuel Morse. Take notes using symbols and abbreviations.

iQ PRACTICE Go online for more practice with using symbols and abbreviations to take notes. *Practice > Unit 4 > Activity 2*

LISTENING 1

OBJECTIVE ▶

Online Friendships

You are going to listen to a lecture about social media and friendship. As you listen, gather information and ideas about how technology affects our relationships.

PREVIEW THE LISTENING

A. VOCABULARY Here are some words and phrases from Listening 1. Read the definitions. Then complete each sentence with the correct word or phrase.

face-to-face *(adjective phrase / adverb phrase)* close to and looking at someone or something

forever *(adverb)* 🔑 for all time; permanently

friendship *(noun)* 🔑 the state of being friends

headline *(noun)* 🔑 the title of a newspaper or magazine article printed in large letters above the story

meaningful *(adjective)* OPAL useful, important, or interesting

post *(verb)* 🔑 to put information or pictures on a website

privacy 🔑 *(noun)* the state of being free from the attention of the public

relationship *(noun)* 🔑 OPAL a connection between two people or things

🔑 Oxford 3000™ words   **OPAL** Oxford Phrasal Academic Lexicon

1. You don't have to be best friends, but it is important to have a good
   _____ with your coworkers.

2. Dora finished writing the article last night. It's ready to _____
   online.

3. We need curtains on those windows. Without them, we have no _____ in the bedroom.

4. It is hard to discuss some things online. You need a _____ conversation where you can see the other person.

ACADEMIC LANGUAGE

The word *relationship* is often used in academic contexts. Notice that the suffix *-ship* is also used in the noun *friendship*. The suffix *-ship* indicates a state or condition.

OPAL

Oxford Phrasal Academic Lexicon

5. His _____ with Tom is very important to Reza. They have known each other for many years.

6. The newspaper _____ said that there will be bad snowstorms in the Midwest today.

7. Their family has lived here _____. I mean a very long time, more than 100 years.

8. The lecturer made some very _____ statements about social media. It gave me a lot to think about.

iQ PRACTICE Go online for more practice with the vocabulary.
Practice > Unit 4 > Activities 3–4

B. PREVIEW You are going to listen to a lecture about social media and friendship. Work with a partner. List one good thing and one possible problem related to social media and friendships.

WORK WITH THE LISTENING

A. LISTEN AND TAKE NOTES Listen to Part 1 of the lecture. The speaker mentions three points that will be in the lecture. Prepare a piece of paper to take notes. List the three points and leave space for writing after each one.

iQ RESOURCES Go online to download extra vocabulary support.
Resources > Extra Vocabulary > Unit 4

B. LISTEN AND TAKE NOTES Listen to Part 2 of the lecture. Take notes. Use symbols and abbreviations to save time.

C. INTERPRET Check (✓) the three sentences that best express the main ideas of the lecture. Use your notes to help you.

☐ 1. Most people will continue to use social media to communicate with friends.

☐ 2. Robin Dunbar usually prefers talking to friends face-to-face, not online.

☐ 3. Some users of social media visit the sites several times each day.

☐ 4. The use of social media is changing the way people think about friendship.

☐ 5. Sixty-nine percent of adults in the United States have online friends.

☐ 6. One danger of social media is that users can lose control of private information.

D. APPLY Listen to Part 2 again. Write the correct number to complete each sentence.

1. In 2018, _____ percent of people in the United States between the ages of 18 and 29 used social media.

2. Worldwide, about _____ people used social media.

3. The speaker says that no one can have meaningful relationships with _____ people.

4. Robin Dunbar did a study of more than _____ people.

5. Most people in this group had about _____ online friends.

6. Of this number of online friends, usually fewer than _____ were close friends.

E. EVALUATE Think about the speaker in Listening 1. Would this person agree or disagree with the following statements? Do you agree or disagree with them? Complete the chart using *A* (agree) or *D* (disagree).

Statement	Speaker	You
1. Online friends aren't real friends.		
2. People should never post personal information online.		
3. Social media can be fun and useful if used carefully.		

F. **EXPLAIN** Compare answers with a partner. Are your answers the same or different? Explain and discuss.

 CRITICAL THINKING STRATEGY

Curiosity

Curiosity is a desire to know or to learn something. Critical thinking requires a curious mind. This means that curious learners do not accept everything they hear as true just because the speaker said it. They also want to know more about the speaker's topic. They ask questions that might start like this:

What did you mean when you said . . . ?

Why did you say that . . . ?

Do you have more information about . . . ?

Where did the statistic about ____ come from?

iQ PRACTICE Go online to watch the Critical Thinking Video and check your comprehension. *Practice > Unit 4 > Activity 5*

 G. **CREATE** Listen again to part of Listening 1. Write two questions you would like to ask the speaker.

1. _____

2. _____

H. **EXTEND** Work with a partner. Share the questions you created in Activity G. How do you think the speaker might answer them? Discuss.

iQ PRACTICE Go online for additional listening and comprehension. *Practice > Unit 4 > Activity 6*

 # SAY WHAT YOU THINK

DISCUSS Discuss the questions in a small group.

1. Were you surprised about the number of people who use social media? Why or why not?

2. How do you think that social media might affect friendships?

3. What are some problems you or your friends experience with social media sites?

LISTENING SKILL Listening for specific information

Sometimes you need to listen for a specific piece of information. To listen for **specific information**, focus on key words. The answer to a question is often just before or after a key word from the question.

You need to know: How many social media users were there worldwide in 2018?

The key word: worldwide

☐ **You hear: Worldwide**, about **2.62 billion** people used social media in 2018.

The answer: 2.62 billion

 A. IDENTIFY Read the questions. Then listen to the statements from Listening 1. Focus on the key words. Answer the questions.

TIP FOR SUCCESS

Practice listening in English as often as possible. At times, you may only understand a few words, but even this can improve your skills.

1. What is the **average number** of friends each person had in Dunbar's study?

_____

2. What was **the point of** the newspaper article with the **headline**, "Nobody has real friends anymore."

_____

3. How did some users compare **online discussions** with ones they had **face-to-face**?

_____

 B. IDENTIFY Read the questions and focus on the words in bold. Listen to a short talk about a photographer named Tanja Hollander. Listen for the bold words to find the information.

1. When Tanja **counted** her online friends, what was the **grand total**?

_____

2. Where **were these friends from**?

_____

3. What did Tanja **decide** to do?

_____

4. How many **years** did it take her to complete her project?

_____

5. **Where** did she go to visit an old college friend, the **poet and hip-hop artist**?

_____

Tanja Hollander

iQ PRACTICE Go online for more practice listening for specific information.
Practice > Unit 4 > Activity 7

Who Are You Talking To?

OBJECTIVE ▶

You are going to listen to a conversation about electronic devices that "talk" to us. As you listen, gather information and ideas about how technology affects our relationships.

PREVIEW THE LISTENING

VOCABULARY SKILL REVIEW

In Unit 3, you learned about synonyms. Some of the correct answers in Activity A are one-word synonyms for the underlined words. Can you identify at least three of these synonyms?

A. VOCABULARY Here are some words and phrases from Listening 2. Read the sentences. Then choose the answer that best matches the meaning of each <u>underlined</u> word or phrase.

1. Since the camera on my smartphone is so good, I rarely use a separate <u>digital</u> camera these days.

   a. easy to carry   b. using computer technology

2. I'm not going to wear that <u>silly</u> hat! Everyone will laugh.

   a. ugly   b. crazy

3. When we got home, we <u>found</u> that the front door was open and our TV was gone!

   a. discovered   b. thought

4. Ronnie sometimes has rather <u>strange</u> ideas about how to do things.

   a. unusual   b. bad

5. I closed my eyes during that part of the movie. It was too <u>scary</u>.

   a. boring   b. frightening

6. The American robin is a <u>common</u> bird. You see them frequently in the spring, summer, and fall.

   a. pretty   b. usual

7. We've become very <u>dependent on</u> our computers in the workplace. We can't function without them.

    a. needing something   b. unhappy about

8. I've <u>disconnected</u> the cable TV in our house. We were watching it too much.

    a. repaired a problem with   b. stopped the service for

iQ PRACTICE   Go online for more practice with the vocabulary.
Practice › Unit 4 › Activities 8–9

B. PREVIEW In the twenty-first century, more and more people use digital devices in their daily lives. Some digital assistants can even "talk" to us. You are going to listen to a conversation that includes a discussion of GPS trackers in cars. Have you used a GPS for driving directions? Discuss with a partner.

WORK WITH THE LISTENING

TIP FOR SUCCESS

When listening, take very short notes to help you remember what you hear. Write only single words or short phrases. Then complete your notes later.

A. CREATE The words and phrases below are key words in the conversation. Think of an abbreviation you can use for each one when you take notes.

1. artificial voices   _____

2. artificial intelligence   _____

3. voice-activated device   _____

4. smart devices   _____

5. too dependent on   _____

6. invention   _____

B. LISTEN AND TAKE NOTES Listen to the conversation and take notes. Use the abbreviations you listed in Activity A.

C. IDENTIFY Choose the description that best summarizes all the main ideas of the conversation.

_____ 1. Digital devices that speak to us are taking the place of the people in our lives by doing things for us and talking with us.

_____ 2. Digital devices can be helpful, but we should remember that they are not human.

_____ 3. Digital devices improve our lives by doing things like giving us directions, doing tasks around the house, and helping people feel less lonely.

D. EXPLAIN Answer the questions. Use your notes to help you. Then listen again and check your answers.

1. Why is Leo frustrated with the GPS voice?

_____

2. What does Aran say about artificial voices?

_____

3. What does Aran's daughter ask the device she calls "Susie" in their home?

_____

4. What is one task in the home that a voice-activated device can do?

_____

5. What did Leo's friends do when they found the device talking to itself?

_____

6. What other invention does Leo mention that changed how people live?

_____

E. EVALUATE Read the descriptions of things mentioned in the conversation. Is the effect of each one on our lives positive, negative, or both? What's your opinion? Add the letter for each item to one section of the Venn diagram.

a. a GPS that gives spoken directions to drivers

b. devices that answer your questions out loud

c. devices that children play games with and talk to

d. digital assistants that perform tasks around the home

e. devices that seem to act independently, such as talking by themselves

f. digital voices that make people feel less lonely

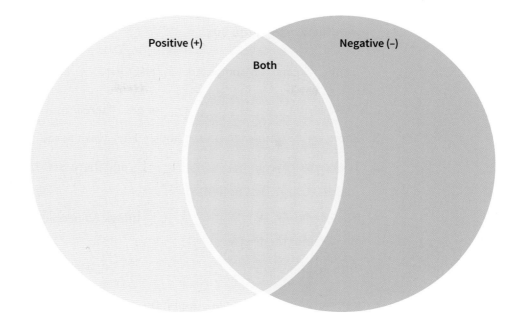

Positive (+)   Both   Negative (–)

F. INTERPRET Compare answers with a partner. Are your opinions similar or different? Give reasons for your opinions.

WORK WITH THE VIDEO

A. PREVIEW What was life like in your country 100 years ago? How was it different from life today?

VIDEO VOCABULARY

heat (v.) to become or to make something hot or warm

candle (n.) a stick of solid wax with a string through the middle, which you can burn to give light

iQ RESOURCES Go online to watch the video about life in Wales in 1927.
Resources > Video > Unit 4 > Unit Video

B. APPLY Watch the video two or three times. Then complete the sentences with the words in the box.

| buy | cars | computers | electricity | kitchen | make | walk |

1. There is no _____ or gas. There is only a fire in the kitchen.

2. There are no bathrooms in the house. They wash in the _____.

3. They don't have _____, and there is no bus. The men have to _____ to work.

4. It's not easy to _____ things, so people _____ many things themselves.

5. With no phones or _____, they have to make their own music.

C. EXTEND Watch the video again. Discuss the questions.

1. Do you think the participants in this program found this life easy or difficult? Why or why not?

2. What did the participants learn from the experiment?

SAY WHAT YOU THINK

SYNTHESIZE Think about the unit video, Listening 1, and Listening 2 as you discuss the questions.

1. Think about one new electronic device that you use frequently. Did this device change your life or your relationships? If so, how? If not, why not?

2. How dependent are you on electronic devices or other modern technology, such as cars or washing machines? Do you know how to manage without them?

3. Would you like to spend two or three months living without any modern technology? Why or why not?

Finding new words in a **dictionary** can be difficult. Sometimes you hear the word, but you don't see it. You may not know how to spell it. This can make it difficult to look up words. Try these ideas to help you.

- Sound out the word and write it down as you say it.

- Think about other spellings of the sounds. For example, think of the word *character*. The sound /k/ can be written as *k*, *c*, *ch*, or *qu*.

- Watch out for double letters. For example, you won't find *occasion* under words beginning with *oca*.

- If you can guess the meaning of the word, look up a synonym in the dictionary. You may find the word in the definition.

- If you have a computer, type the word as you hear it and then use the spell-check function. The computer may correct it for you.

Note: Some words have "silent letters." For example, the *k* in *know* and the *l* in *walk* are both silent.

 A. VOCABULARY Listen to the sentences. At the end of each sentence, the speaker is going to repeat one word from the sentence. Guess the spelling of each word. Then try to look up each one in your dictionary. Use one or more of the ideas from the Vocabulary Skill box.

TIP FOR SUCCESS

With online dictionaries and indexes, it is no longer necessary to know how to use alphabetical order to find things. However, this is still a useful skill. Take some time to learn the rules for alphabetical order in order to find items in a print dictionary or index.

My guess	Correct spelling
1.	
2.	
3.	
4.	
5.	

B. DISCUSS Work with a partner. Compare your answers in Activity A. Then discuss the questions.

1. Which words were hard to find in the dictionary? Why?

2. Were there any words you did not find? If so, which ones?

3. Which ideas did you use to look for the words in Activity A? Which ideas do you think you are going to use in the future?

iQ PRACTICE Go online for more practice using the dictionary.
Practice › Unit 4 › Activity 10

SPEAKING

OBJECTIVE ▶ At the end of this unit, you are going to take part in a panel discussion about the effects of social media on society. After the discussion, your classmates may ask you to clarify some of your statements or ideas. After you listen to your classmates' discussions, ask questions to clarify things you don't understand.

GRAMMAR Comparatives

We use **comparatives** to talk about the differences between two things. Comparatives often use *than* to connect the two things being compared. Comparatives can be either positive or negative.

To make a **positive comparative,** follow the rules below for one-syllable adjectives. For two-syllable words, use *more* before the adjective or adverb.

> Our lives are becoming **more public than** they were in the past.
> Online arguments are often **angrier than** face-to-face ones.
> Jon will get the message **more quickly** if you send it to his phone.

For **negative comparatives**, use *less* before the adjective or adverb.

> Our lives are becoming **less private**.
> Many people think online discussions are **less respectful than** face-to-face discussions.

These are the basic rules for forming comparative adjectives.

Rule	Adjective	Comparative
Add *-er* to one-syllable adjectives.	cheap	cheap**er**
Delete final *-e* before adding *-er*.	close	clos**er**
Some two-syllable adjectives take *-er*.	quiet	quiet**er**
Change final *y* to *i* before adding *-er*.	easy	eas**ier**
Double the final consonant when the word ends with a single vowel and a consonant. Then add *-er*.	big	big**ger**
Use *more* or *less* with adjectives that have two or more syllables.	creative	**more** creative **less** creative
Some adjectives have irregular comparative forms.	good bad	**better** **worse**

iQ RESOURCES Go online to watch the Grammar Skill Video.
Resources > Video > Unit 4 > Grammar Skill Video

A. APPLY Complete each sentence with a positive (+) or negative (–) comparative. Use the adjective or adverb in parentheses.

1. Studies have shown that teens who spend a lot of time on social media are
_____ (lonely +) than teens who spend less time.

2. Using social media makes it _____ (easy +) to stay in touch
with friends.

3. Now that I'm using the GPS, I get lost _____ (often –) than
I used to.

4. After interacting with digital voices, some people felt _____
(lonely –) than before.

5. I'm becoming _____ (dependent +) on my smartphone
every day.

6. Voice-activated devices are becoming _____ (common +) in
our homes.

B. CREATE Complete each sentence with a comparative that expresses your opinion. Use the adjective in parentheses. Then discuss with a partner.

1. Sending a birthday card to someone online is _____ (meaningful) than sending a card in the mail.

2. Face-to-face conversations are _____ (interesting) than online conversations.

3. I sometimes think that my smartphone is _____ (intelligent) than I am.

4. Protecting my privacy online is _____ (important) to me than having a lot of online friends.

iQ PRACTICE Go online for more practice with comparatives.
Practice > Unit 4 > Activity 11

iQ PRACTICE Go online for the Grammar Expansion: order of adjectives.
Practice > Unit 4 > Activity 12

PRONUNCIATION Linking between consonant sounds

Sometimes one word ends and the following word begins with the same consonant sound. In this case, speakers often hold the first sound and **link** it to the next. They don't repeat the consonant sound. Knowing this will improve your comprehension and help you to speak more easily and fluently.

We turn everything off and do things like play games.

How does technology affect our relationships?

Note: When a word ends in silent *e*, the sound of the last consonant is still linked to the next word.

I have very good relationships with my online friends.

A. IDENTIFY Listen to the sentences. Mark the link between consonants in each sentence. Then listen again and repeat.

1. Perhaps you should stop putting so much personal information online.

2. I read an online newspaper every morning.

3. He's putting up his website tomorrow.

4. Could you please take care of that for me?

5. In Dunbar's study, the average number of online friends was 150.

B. **ANALYZE** Work with a partner. Mark the links between consonants in each sentence. Then practice saying the sentences.

1. Don't delete too much information.

2. I think that *Are You Really My Friend?* is a great title for Tanja Hollander's book.

3. Let me make just one quick comment about that.

4. I have some more statistics about the number of users.

5. She received nine new friend requests yesterday.

iQ PRACTICE   Go online for more practice with links between consonant sounds. *Practice* ❯ *Unit 4* ❯ *Activity 13*

SPEAKING SKILL   Asking for and giving clarification

Ask for **clarification** when you don't understand something.

Sometimes you can ask for clarification by repeating something the speaker has said and using question intonation. In Listening 2, Aran is surprised when Leo says his friends disconnected their device. He repeats the phrase with question intonation. Then Leo explains.

> **Aran:** What did they do?
> **Leo:** They disconnected it.
> **Aran:** Disconnected it?
> **Leo:** Yes, completely.

You can also use questions like these to ask for clarification.

> Could you explain . . . ?
> What do you mean? / Do you mean . . . ?
> What does _____ mean?
> What's a/an _____?

Use phrases like these to give clarification.

> What I mean is . . .
> What I'm saying is . . .
> That's right.
> That's not what I meant.
> Let me explain.

A. IDENTIFY Work with a partner. Read the excerpts from Listening 2. Underline the phrases the speakers use to ask for and give clarification.

1. **Leo:** Do you mean because people like me are beginning to interact with them as if they were real humans?

   Aran: That's right. It's almost as if the machines are becoming our friends.

2. **Aran:** In a way, it's nice to have all of these "smart" devices that can do things for us, but I think we need to be careful about how we use them.

   Leo: Be careful? What do you mean?

   Aran: What I'm saying is that we shouldn't become too dependent on these things.

B. CREATE Work in a small group. Follow these steps.

1. Choose a topic from the box or use your own idea.

   - Something I enjoy doing online
   - Something I prefer to do in person
   - An interesting website I recently visited
   - Why I want/don't want a digital assistant

2. Make some notes about your topic.

3. Speak to the group for one minute about your topic. When a listener asks for clarification, explain your idea again.

4. Listen to the other members of the group. When you don't understand something, ask for clarification.

iQ PRACTICE Go online for more practice with asking for and giving clarification. *Practice > Unit 4 > Activity 14*

UNIT ASSIGNMENT **Have a panel discussion about social media**

OBJECTIVE ▶

In this section, you are going to work in a group to have a panel discussion about social media. As you prepare for your discussion, think about the Unit Question, "How does technology affect our relationships?" Use information from Listening 1, Listening 2, the unit video, and your work in this unit to support your presentation. Refer to the Self-Assessment checklist on page 88.

CONSIDER THE IDEAS

 INVESTIGATE Listen to the speaker introduce your panel discussion about social media and society. What are the three topics the speaker mentions? Write them below. Then think of one more possible topic of your own.

Topic 1: _____

Topic 2: _____

Topic 3: _____

Topic 4: _____

PREPARE AND SPEAK

A. GATHER IDEAS **Work in a small group.**

1. Discuss the question "Are social media sites good or bad for society?" Use the topics from Consider the Ideas as a guide, including one additional topic based on suggestions in Activity B. List as many pros (arguments for) and cons (arguments against) for each topic as you can.

2. Don't say "no" to any ideas yet. This is a process known as *brainstorming*. Take notes. Use symbols and abbreviations in order to write more quickly.

TIP FOR SUCCESS

Brainstorming is a way of producing ideas by holding an informal group discussion.

B. ORGANIZE IDEAS **With your group, review notes from Activity A.**

1. Choose the best ideas to create a chart like the one below, with a *Topic* column and columns for pros and cons.

Topic	Pros	Cons
Business		

2. Try to have an equal number of pros and cons. Use comparative forms whenever possible.

3. Organize the discussion. Make sure that each member of the group has a part.

C. SPEAK Practice your panel discussion. Then present the discussion to the class (or to another group). Refer to the Self-Assessment checklist below before you begin. After your discussion, invite classmates to ask questions about anything they didn't understand. Clarify and explain.

iQ PRACTICE Go online for your alternate Unit Assignment.
Practice > Unit 4 > Activity 15

CHECK AND REFLECT

A. CHECK Think about the Unit Assignment as you complete the Self-Assessment checklist.

SELF-ASSESSMENT	Yes	No
I was able to speak easily about the topic.	☐	☐
I used symbols and abbreviations in my notes.	☐	☐
My group or class understood me.	☐	☐
I used positive and negative comparatives correctly.	☐	☐
I used vocabulary from the unit.	☐	☐
I asked for and gave clarification.	☐	☐
I used links between consonant sounds.	☐	☐

B. REFLECT Discuss these questions with a partner or group.

1. What is something new you learned in this unit?

2. Look back at the Unit Question—How does technology affect our relationships? Is your answer different now than when you started this unit? If yes, how is it different? Why?

iQ PRACTICE Go to the online discussion board to discuss the questions.
Practice > Unit 4 > Activity 16

TRACK YOUR SUCCESS

iQ PRACTICE Go online to check the words and phrases you have learned in this unit. *Practice > Unit 4 > Activity 17*

Check (✓) the skills and strategies you learned. If you need more work on a skill, refer to the page(s) in parentheses.

NOTE-TAKING	☐ I can use symbols and abbreviations to take notes. (p. 70)
CRITICAL THINKING	☐ I can use my curiosity. (p. 74)
LISTENING	☐ I can listen for specific information. (p. 75)
VOCABULARY	☐ I can use the dictionary to find new words. (p. 81)
GRAMMAR	☐ I can use comparatives. (p. 82)
PRONUNCIATION	☐ I can link consonant sounds. (p. 84)
SPEAKING	☐ I can ask for and give clarification. (p. 85)

OBJECTIVE ▶ ☐ I can gather information and ideas to make a presentation about the effects of social media on society.

5 Sociology

NOTE-TAKING	using a simple outline
LISTENING	listening for reasons and explanations
CRITICAL THINKING	ranking
VOCABULARY	word families: verbs, nouns, adjectives
GRAMMAR	auxiliary verbs in questions
PRONUNCIATION	intonation in questions with *or*
SPEAKING	expressing opinions

What does it mean to be part of a family?

A. Discuss these questions with your classmates.

1. What is your definition of a family?

2. Which members of your family influence your life? How?

3. Look at the photo. Who do you think the people are?

B. Listen to *The Q Classroom* online. Then choose the correct phrases from the box to complete the sentences.

   a. don't have good relationships

   b. family has to come first

   c. for these people, friends are their family

   d. she always has her family

   e. you aren't alone

1. Yuna says that being part of a family means that __d__.

2. Marcus agrees with Yuna and says it also means that __b__.

3. Sophy thinks being part of a family means that __e__.

4. Felix says that some people __a__ with family members.

5. Because of this, Felix says that __c__.

iQ PRACTICE Go to the online discussion board to discuss the Unit Question with your classmates. *Practice > Unit 5 > Activity 1*

UNIT OBJECTIVE	Listen to an interview and a lecture. Gather information and ideas to give a speech about families.

[handwritten notes: don't live with me; grand family; extended family; father mother; unclear family]

Using an outline is one way of keeping notes organized. You can make a simple outline based on questions and answers. Sometimes, a speaker will begin by stating the questions he or she will answer, as in this example.

> Today I'm going to talk about the family. What were families like in the past? How are families changing today? And finally, what will the family be like in the future?

In a case like this, you can make an outline by writing short notes about the questions and leaving space after each one to write notes about the speaker's comments.

How are family here different from family in other country?

why are they different?

what do they have in common?

The Family
A   the past
B   changes
C   the future

🔊 **IDENTIFY** Listen to the introduction to a talk about families around the world. Then make a simple question outline that you could use to take notes.

iQ PRACTICE Go online for more practice using a simple outline to take notes. *Practice > Unit 5 > Activity 2*

LISTENING 1

Personality → (R)
characthistic → (E١)

Twins in the Family

OBJECTIVE ▶

You are going to listen to an interview with psychologist Dr. Mona Bashir. Dr. Bashir talks about twins and their life in the family. As you listen, gather information and ideas about what it means to be part of a family.

Monday

PREVIEW THE LISTENING

A. VOCABULARY Here are some words from Listening 1. Read the paragraphs. Then write each <u>underlined</u> word next to the correct definition.

My friends Layla and Manar are <u>twins</u>! They have exactly the same physical <u>appearance</u>. Their eyes, their hair, and even their noses look the same. Twins <u>inherit</u> the same hair and eye color from their parents. Sometimes twins even act very much alike. Layla and Manar live in different cities. Yesterday, they both went shopping for shoes. They both bought the same kind of shoes. They were the same color, style, and brand. That was an amazing <u>coincidence</u>. They didn't plan to buy the same shoes. It just happened!

Incident (n)
"
happaning

inheritence (v)

1. ___coincidence___ (*noun*) two things that happen at the same time by chance
2. ___appearance___ (*noun*) the way someone looks
3. ___inherit___ (*verb*) to get a characteristic from your parents
4. ___twins___ (*noun*) two children born to the same mother at the same time

I am very close to my sister, Louise. We aren't twins, but I am only one year younger than she is. As children, we had a <u>tendency</u> to do everything together. When I was ready to go to college, I wanted to go to the same university as Louise. But our parents didn't agree with that idea. They felt we each needed to develop our own <u>identity</u>. Now Louise is married and has her own family. We have <u>separate</u> lives, but we still <u>get along</u> very well and enjoy doing things together.

5. _____sepavet_____ (*adjective*) different; not connected

6. _____tendency_____ (*noun*) something a person usually does

7. _____identity_____ (*noun*) who or what a person or thing is

8. _____get along_____ (*verb phrase*) to have a friendly relationship with someone

iQ PRACTICE Go online for more practice with the vocabulary.
Practice > Unit 5 > Activities 3–4

B. PREVIEW You are going to listen to an interview about twins. What do you think psychologist Dr. Mona Bashir will say about twins? Circle your choice.

a. Twins should share everything and be in the same classes at school.

b. Twins need to be able to develop their own individual personalities.

WORK WITH THE LISTENING

A. LISTEN AND TAKE NOTES Listen to Part 1 of the interview. The interviewer asks Dr. Bashir some questions. Use a simple outline with question notes to take notes about the answers.

twins – What physical differences? Hight is defferent

personalities? – Like same things or different? team / Teniss - music

How twins relate to family? get along with anther brother

what diffrence between her twins?

B. INVESTIGATE Listen to Part 2 of the interview. Again, the interviewer asks questions. Take notes about the questions and answers. *personal → 1 team sports*

2 7=2 topi

C. IDENTIFY Listen to the whole interview. Add more information to your notes. Then read the questions and choose the correct answers.

1. What does Dr. Bashir say about the differences and similarities between her twin boys? *→ can speak with out talking*

   a. There are small differences in their appearance and personalities.

   b. Faris is very social and likes sports, but Fahad is quiet and likes music. *→ they understand each other*

   c. There are no differences in their physical appearance.

2. How is the twins' relationship with their older brother different from their relationship with each other?

   a. They don't get along with their brother because they can't communicate.

   b. They can communicate with their brother by just looking at him.

   c. They get along with their brother, but their own relationship is closer.

3. What does the example of the Springer-Lewis twins show about twins raised in different families?

   a. They have problems later in life.

   b. They are very different from their families.

   c. They can be very similar to each other.

4. What conclusion does Dr. Bashir make based on this story and her own experience?

   a. Our personalities are formed by chance and have no connection to our family.

   b. Our personalities are formed by both inherited tendencies and family influence.

   c. Our personalities are formed by our life experiences. We don't inherit them.

D. RESTATE Answer the questions. Use your notes to help you. Then listen again and check your answers.

1. Which twin is taller, Faris or Fahad?

   _____

2. What sports do Faris and Fahad like to play?

   _____ *soccer* ___ *tennis music* _____

3. How did the twins communicate when they were babies?

   _____ *baby talk* ___ *look each other* _____ *each other*

   own langages to undentand

4. What did Dr. Bashir and her husband do when the boys started first grade?

_____ put different class school _____

5. Why did they do this? to devepot to

need separete life _____

6. How do Faris and Fahad feel when they are together?

_____ together like one person _____

7. What two things did both of the Springer-Lewis twins like?

make coming wood dag's name and wife name

math

8. What two small coincidences did Dr. Bashir mention in relation to the Springer-Lewis twins?

_____

E. EVALUATE Do you think Dr. Bashir agrees or disagrees with these statements? Write *A* (agree) or *D* (disagree).

___D___ 1. It is a good idea for parents to dress twins in the same clothes.

___A___ 2. It is a good thing for twins to have different interests and friends sometimes.

___D___ 3. Twins often don't get along very well with other children in the family.

___A___ 4. Although they are similar in many ways, twins will usually have some differences in their appearance and personality.

___D___ 5. We are not born with any certain personality. Personality comes from our life experiences in the family and outside.

F. EVALUATE Work in a group. Compare your answers to Activity E. Then discuss the answers that are different.

iQ PRACTICE Go online for additional listening and comprehension.
Practice > Unit 5 > Activity 5

SAY WHAT YOU THINK

DISCUSS Discuss the questions in a group.

1. Which do you think has more influence on your personality: characteristics you inherit or people and events in your life? Why?

2. Think of the coincidences in the Springer-Lewis twins' lives. What are some coincidences among people you know?

3. Look at the photo of adult twins on page 96. How do you think they are different from each other as adults?

LISTENING SKILL Listening for reasons and explanations

Good speakers give **reasons** and **explanations** to support what they say. When you hear a speaker make a statement about something or express an opinion, it's important to ask yourself, "Why did the speaker say this?" Then listen for reasons or an explanation. Look at this example from "Twins in the Family."

> **Statement:** Starting in the first grade, we decided to put them [the twins] in different classes in school.

Question to ask yourself: Why did they put the twins in different classes?

> **Reasons:** They had different teachers and school friends. These experiences helped them develop their own personalities.

A. EXPLAIN Listen to the interview again. Answer the questions.

TIP FOR SUCCESS
In a conversation, look at the person who is speaking. Focus on what the person is saying. You will understand more.

1. Why does Faris prefer to play soccer rather than tennis?

   _____ He's social _____

2. Why do the twins feel like different people when they are apart?

   _____ treat them differently _____

B. IDENTIFY Listen to the radio call-in show. Complete the statements.

1. Hal probably feels closer to his friends than his family because ___ friends ___ are less critical, family is tell you do and thing saying wrong thing

2. Marielena thinks family members are more critical than friends because _____ don't think your problem is mine, _____

---

iQ PRACTICE Go online for more practice with listening for reasons and explanations. *Practice > Unit 5 > Activity 6*

LISTENING 2 Family History

OBJECTIVE ▶

You are going to listen to a lecturer describe how a group of famous African Americans used DNA to learn about their family history. As you listen, gather information and ideas about what it means to be part of a family.

PREVIEW THE LISTENING

VOCABULARY SKILL REVIEW

In Unit 1, you learned about noun + verb collocations. The noun *record* is often used with the verbs *check* and *destroy*, and one other verb. What verb is *record* used with in this activity?

A. VOCABULARY Here are some words from Listening 2. Read the sentences. Then choose the answer that best matches the meaning of each underlined word.

1. Our assignment is to <u>search</u> for information about where our grandparents were born. I'll go to the library, and you check online.

    a. look for

    b. write down

2. Evelyn's great-great-grandfather was a <u>slave</u> in Georgia. He ran away to Canada.

    a. a person who is free

    b. a person who is owned by another person

3. Our school library has an electronic <u>database</u> with the titles and authors of all
   of the books in the library. You can look at it online. *(n)*

   a. a book of information

   b. information organized and stored in a computer

4. I am very close to my <u>cousin</u> Amal. I often see her when our families get
   together. *(n)*

   a. the child of an aunt or uncle

   b. a very special friend

   turn out → resulted, suprising, to

5. Some of Ron's <u>ancestors</u> on his mother's side of the family came from Italy in
   the 1880s. *(n)*

   a. relatives who lived a long time ago

   b. aunts and uncles

6. We need <u>input</u> from everyone on the team. Adel, what do you think? *(n)*

   a. ideas and information *a lot*

   b. computer files

ACADEMIC LANGUAGE

The word *input* is
often used in spoken
and written academic
English. It originally
referred to data or
information fed into
computers. Now it also
refers to contributions
of ideas or information
in any situation. *Kayla
gave us valuable **input**
during our discussion.*

_____ | OPAL
Oxford Phrasal Academic Lexicon

7. Alfredo was never an active <u>participant</u> in the class, so most students didn't like
   being in his group. He did not like to practice speaking. *(n)*

   a. someone who teaches a class

   b. someone who takes part in something

8. The city keeps <u>records</u> of all the people who were born or died here. They file
   and keep track of them all. *(n)*

   a. files of information

   b. disks with music on them

iQ PRACTICE Go online for more practice with the vocabulary.
Practice › Unit 5 › Activities 7–8

B. PREVIEW You are going to listen to a lecture about how a group of people
used DNA to learn about their family history. Write two questions you
would like to ask about your own family history.

1. 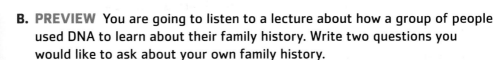 _____

2. _____

WORK WITH THE LISTENING

A. LISTEN AND TAKE NOTES The speaker in this lecture often makes statements and then gives reasons and explanations to explain them. Listen and take notes about the explanations for these statements.

Most African Americans have little information about their ancestors.

come to US As slaves / few written records

Henry Louis Gates used DNA to study the history of African-American families. *どこから きたか? what part of AA came from, who*

The results of Gates's study were surprising. *びっくり uncomfotable*

50% black   50 white — アイデンティ   some peopo

Another person in Gates's study, author Bliss Broyard, had a different experience. *look   before that*

hid white family   じぶん アフロが多く

80% black

DNP だけじゃない / 生活もある

B. INVESTIGATE Work with a partner. Review and edit your notes. Then listen again and add more information.

C. EVALUATE Check (✓) the sentence that best states the main idea of the lecture.

____ 1. You need to know your family history to know who you really are.

____ 2. Our genes and our family history form part of our identity, but they don't tell the whole story.

____ 3. Some participants were surprised to discover how many of their ancestors came from places other than Africa.

D. IDENTIFY Read the questions. Choose the correct answers. Use your notes to help you. Then listen and check your answers.

1. What is one reason that some African Americans have little information about their family history?

a. Their ancestors came to America as slaves.

b. They weren't interested in family history.

c. Their grandparents never told them family stories.

2. Who is Henry Louis Gates?

a. a scientist

b. a historian

c. a journalist

3. What new tool did Henry Louis Gates use in his study of the African-Americans' families?

a. newspaper stories

b. books and public records

c. DNA

4. What does it mean when two people have the same "markers" in their DNA?

a. They are brothers or sisters.

b. They are not related.

c. They have a common ancestor.

5. Where did some of Henry Louis Gates's ancestors come from?

a. Ireland

b. Scotland

c. England

6. What percentage of Bliss Broyard's DNA comes from her African ancestors?

a. 15 percent

b. 18 percent

c. 50 percent

E. APPLY Work with a partner. Read the excerpt from Listening 2 and try to fill in the missing words. Then listen and check your answers.

Some people have little information about their _____ancestors_____.
                                                        1

For example, the ancestors of most African Americans came to America as

_____slaves_____. There are very few _____written_____ records of
       2   3

their family _____history_____, especially before they came to America.
                    4

For this _____reason_____, historian Henry Louis Gates recently used
              5

_____DNA_____ to study the family history of several famous African
     6

Americans. _____participants_____ in the study wanted to know what
                    7

_____part_____ of Africa their families came from. Who were their
       8

African ancestors?

CRITICAL THINKING STRATEGY

Ranking

To **rank** means to put things in order using certain criteria. A **criterion** (plural *criteria*) is a standard that you use when you make a decision or form an opinion about someone or something. In some cases, the choice of criteria is up to you. For example, you can rank books from those you like most to those you like least. This would be useful when cleaning out your bookshelves. Sometimes we need to rank things based on more fact-based criteria. For example, restaurant rankings are often based on things like price, how clean they are, or service.

iQ PRACTICE   Go online to watch the Critical Thinking Video and check your comprehension. *Practice › Unit 5 › Activity 9*

F. APPLY What makes you who you are? Think about ideas from Listening 1 and Listening 2. Then number the items from 1 to 6 in order of importance for you (1 = most important, 6 = least important). Remember that in this example, there are no right or wrong answers.

Rank	Items
	My family now
	My DNA
	My education
	The country I live in
	My family history
	Other life experiences

G. EXPLAIN Work with a partner and compare your answers. Are they similar or different? Explain your choices.

WORK WITH THE VIDEO

 A. PREVIEW What can a person learn by traveling to another country?

iQ RESOURCES Go online to watch the video about a woman who travels to visit her family. *Resources > Video > Unit 5 > Unit Video*

VIDEO VOCABULARY

chef (n.) a person who works as the chief cook in a restaurant

knock (v.) to make a noise by hitting something

mutton (n.) the meat from an adult sheep

curry (n.) a dish with meat, vegetables, and many spices popular in India and other Asian countries

B. ANALYZE Watch the video again. Choose the correct answers.

1. How did Nadiya become a famous chef?
   a. by working in a restaurant   b. by winning a TV baking competition

2. Where did she grow up?
   a. in the UK   b. in Bangladesh

3. How does she feel about her nationality?
   a. very Bangladeshi   b. very British

4. Why is Nadiya's family celebrating in the UK?
   a. She won a baking competition.   b. She's traveling to Bangladesh.

5. What is one reason Nadiya wants to go to Bangladesh?
   a. to learn about the culture and food   b. to learn about life in a big city

6. Why does Nadiya cry when she sees her family in Bangladesh?
   a. They aren't happy to see her.   b. She realizes she missed them.

C. DISCUSS Ask and answer the questions with a partner.

1. In the video, we're told that Nadiya's grandmother is very important to her. Why do you think this is so?

2. What do you think Nadiya will learn from the rest of her travels in Bangladesh? How will the experience change her?

SAY WHAT YOU THINK

SYNTHESIZE Think about the unit video, Listening 1, and Listening 2 as you discuss the questions.

1. Many families in the world today have family members who live in different countries. How does this affect family life? What are the advantages and disadvantages?

2. How important is it to keep in touch with your larger family, that is aunts, uncles, cousins, grandparents, and so on?

3. Who has been an important person in your life? It might be a family member or other person. Why is the person important?

VOCABULARY SKILL Word families: verbs, nouns, adjectives

Word families are groups of words usually based on the same *root* or *headword*. When you learn a new word, try to learn different forms of the word at the same time. You can often find word families listed together in dictionaries.

verb	noun	adjective
inform	information	informative

iQ RESOURCES Go online to watch the Vocabulary Skill Video.
Resources ＞ Video ＞ Unit 3 ＞ Vocabulary Skill Video

A. CATEGORIZE Complete the chart with other forms of the words. Use a dictionary to help you.

Verb	Noun	~~Adjective~~ *Adverb*	*Adjective*
participate	participant	participatory	
coincide	*coincidence*	*coincidently*	*coincident*
differ	*difference*	*differently*	*different*
identify	*Identification*	*identifing*	
tend	*tendency*		

(handwritten left margin: run into, bumped-in to (T))

(handwritten: an Apple & an Orange differ from each other [from] in their color size.)

B. APPLY Complete each sentence with the correct word from Activity A. Use a dictionary to check your answers.

1. I can't __identify__ the person in this old photo. Is that my grandfather or his brother?

2. Everyone in my mother's family has a(n) __tendency__ to be very thin. It's in their DNA, I guess.

3. My sister and I look very __different__ from one another. I'm blond and blue-eyed, but she has dark hair and brown eyes.

4. Amy was a(n) __participant__ in the study group. She thought the experience was worth her time. She was glad to help.

5. I was on the bus the other day, and I ran into an old friend I haven't seen in years. What a(n) __coincidence__! I didn't know he lived near me.

iQ PRACTICE Go online for more practice with word families.
Practice ＞ Unit 5 ＞ Activity 10

SPEAKING

OBJECTIVE ▶

At the end of this unit, you are going to give a short speech about a quotation related to the idea of family. You will explain the quotation and then give your opinion about it. After listening to classmates' speeches, you will have a chance to ask questions.

GRAMMAR Auxiliary verbs in questions

Most questions in English are formed with an **auxiliary verb**, sometimes called a *helping verb*. This is true for all tenses. The basic pattern in questions is **auxiliary verb + subject + main verb**. This is true for *Yes/No questions* and for *information questions* that begin with question words. Study the examples in the charts. Note that in the *simple present* and *simple past* the main verb is always in base form.

yes/no questions

auxiliary verb	subject	main verb	(rest of sentence)
Did	the twins and their brother	have	a good relationship?
Is	Hal	searching	for his mother?
Do	you	agree	with Chris Rock?

information questions

question word	auxiliary verb	subject	main verb	(rest of sentence)
What	does	it	mean	to be part of a family?
How	can	you	explain	this?
Who	did	Faris	look like?	
Why	do	family members	help	each other?

A. COMPOSE Write *Yes/No* questions with the words.

1. they / study (present) / math at school

   Do they study math at school?

2. your grandfather / come (past) / here from Lebanon in the 1900s

   Did your grandfather come here from Lebanon in the 1900?

3. Andrew / have (present) / a twin brother

   Does Andrew have a twin brother?

4. he / want (present) / to go to Ireland next week

   Does he want to go to Ireland next week?

B. COMPOSE Write information questions with the words.

1. why / Henry Louis Gates / use (past) / DNA in the study

   Why did Henry Louis Gates use DNA in the study?

2. how / you / find out (past) / about your family history

   How did you find out about your family history?

3. who / your son / look like (present)

   Who does your son look like?

4. what / the twins / do (present continuous) / today

   What are the twins diong today?

C. CREATE Work with a partner. Imagine that you are talking to Dr. Bashir in Listening 1 and the speaker in Listening 2. Write two questions you would like to ask each person.

Listening 1: "Twins in the Family"

Yes No 1. _Do you think it's hard to growe up?_

Infor 2. _When can I know I'm pregnant twins?_

Listening 2: "Family History"

Yes No 1. _Do you want to check your family history?_

Inf 2. _what did you think when your ancestor was a slave?_

D. DISCUSS Share your questions with another pair of students. Discuss possible answers.

iQ PRACTICE Go online for more practice with auxiliary verbs in questions.
Practice > Unit 5 > Activities 11–12

Some questions offer the listener two choices. The choices are usually connected with the word *or*. These questions usually have rising-falling **intonation**. This is true for both *Yes/No* and information questions with *or*.

Are we just born that way or is it the influence of our families?

Is the man in the picture your brother or your cousin?

Does your twin brother like the same food as you or different food?

Are you more similar to your mother or your father?

[handwritten notes: mother brother father, sister, のがらコえったり, 父 土いごのせいて]

A. APPLY Listen to the questions. Then repeat them, using the same intonation that you hear.

1. Do you look more like your mother or your father?
2. Which do you think is more important: your DNA or your life experience?
3. Was the meeting a coincidence, or did they plan it?
4. Do you spend more time with your friends or your family?

B. EXTEND Work with a partner. Take turns asking the questions. Practice saying the questions with the correct intonation. Then write two more questions with *or*. Practice saying them.

1. Do you learn faster by reading a book or by listening to a teacher?
2. Which do you use more: a telephone or a computer?
3. Do you like to watch TV at night or read a book?
4. _____
5. _____

iQ PRACTICE Go online for more practice with intonation in questions with *or*.
Practice > Unit 5 > Activity 13

When you express an **opinion**, you usually introduce your idea with words that signal an opinion. This is also true when you are explaining another person's opinion. Look at these examples:

> **In my view**, stories like this show that we are born with a tendency to have certain personality characteristics.
>
> **For me**, friends and family are different, even though I love both.
>
> **I feel that** I now understand more about myself and where I come from.
>
> **In the writer's opinion**, no one should have to have a DNA analysis.

Using phrases like these says to the listener, *"This is an opinion. It's not a fact. You don't have to agree."*

 A. IDENTIFY Listen to the speakers express opinions. Write the phrases they use to introduce their opinions.

1. _I think_
2. _I feel that_
3. _In my view_
4. _for me_
5. _as I see it_

TIP FOR SUCCESS

Opinions are often the main ideas of a speech or presentation. Pay attention to special phrases that signal an opinion. They will help you find main ideas.

B. DISCUSS Work with a partner. Take turns answering the questions and expressing your opinions. Use expressions from the Speaking Skill box and other expressions you know to signal your opinions.

1. Which of these people is more a part of your family: a cousin you never met or your best friend? Why?

2. How do you define the word *home*?

3. "A gram of blood is worth more than a kilogram of friendship" is a Spanish proverb. What does this mean to you?

iQ PRACTICE Go online for more practice with expressing opinions.
Practice › Unit 5 › Activity 14

UNIT ASSIGNMENT   Give a short speech

OBJECTIVE ▶

In this section, you are going to give a short speech about families. As you prepare your speech, think about the Unit Question, "What does it mean to be part of a family?" Use information from Listening 1, Listening 2, the unit video, and your work in this unit to support your speech. Refer to the Self-Assessment checklist on page 110.

CONSIDER THE IDEAS

INVESTIGATE   Read the quotations about families. Then discuss them in a group. What does each quotation mean?

"A family is a unit composed not only of children, but of men, women . . . and the common cold."
– Ogden Nash (poet and humorist, 1902–1971)

"Family isn't about whose blood you have. It's about who you care about."
– Trey Parker and Matt Stone (writers, 1998)

"Happiness is having a large, loving, caring family—in another city."
– George Burns (comedian and writer, 1896–1996)

"A person sometimes needs to separate himself from family and friends and go to new places in order to change."
– Katherine Butler Hathaway (writer, 1890–1942)

PREPARE AND SPEAK

A. GATHER IDEAS   Choose one of the quotations above to create a short speech. Your speech should answer these questions.

1. What do you think the quotation means?

2. Do you agree or disagree with the quotation? Why?

B. ORGANIZE IDEAS   Use the chart to make notes for your speech. Do not write complete sentences in the chart. Take only five minutes to do this.

Quotation	
Meaning of the quotation	
My opinion about the quotation	

C. SPEAK Work in a group. Give a short speech about the quotation you chose. Follow these rules for the speeches. Refer to the Self-Assessment checklist below before you begin.

1. Each person should speak for exactly two minutes—no more and no less.

2. One member of the group keeps track of the time for each speaker. Give the speaker a signal, such as a raised hand, after 1 minute 30 seconds. This means there are just 30 seconds left.

3. If the speaker stops before two minutes, someone in the group should ask a question to help him or her continue.

4. After two minutes, the speaker must stop talking.

D. DISCUSS Ask and answer these questions with your group.

1. How did you feel about giving your speech? Were you nervous or relaxed?

2. Was the speech easy or difficult for you? Why?

3. Did other members of the group understand your speech?

iQ PRACTICE Go online for your alternate Unit Assignment.
Practice > Unit 5 > Activity 15

CHECK AND REFLECT

A. CHECK Think about the Unit Assignment as you complete the Self-Assessment checklist.

SELF-ASSESSMENT	Yes	No
I was able to speak easily about the topic.	☐	☐
My group understood me.	☐	☐
I used auxiliary verbs in questions.	☐	☐
I used vocabulary from the unit.	☐	☐
I expressed my opinion.	☐	☐
I used intonation in questions with *or*.	☐	☐

B. REFLECT Discuss these questions with a partner or group.

1. What is something new you learned in this unit?

2. Look back at the Unit Question—What does it mean to be part of a family? Is your answer different now than when you started this unit? If yes, how is it different? Why?

iQ PRACTICE Go to the online discussion board to discuss the questions.
Practice > Unit 5 > Activity 16

TRACK YOUR SUCCESS

iQ PRACTICE Go online to check the words and phrases you have learned in this unit. *Practice > Unit 5 > Activity 17*

Check (✓) the skills you learned. If you need more work on a skill, refer to the page(s) in parentheses.

NOTE-TAKING	☐ I can use a simple outline to take notes. (p. 92)
LISTENING	☐ I can listen for reasons and explanations. (p. 97)
CRITICAL THINKING	☐ I can make judgments about the importance of information and ideas. (p. 102)
VOCABULARY	☐ I can use verbs, nouns, and adjectives from word families. (p. 104)
GRAMMAR	☐ I can use auxiliary verbs in questions. (p. 105)
PRONUNCIATION	☐ I can use intonation in questions with *or*. (p. 107)
SPEAKING	☐ I can express opinions. (p. 108)
OBJECTIVE ▶	☐ I can gather information and ideas to give a speech about families.

Behavioral Science

NOTE-TAKING	reviewing and editing notes
LISTENING	listening for dates and other numbers
CRITICAL THINKING	identifying "false" inferences
VOCABULARY	word families: suffixes
GRAMMAR	imperative verbs
PRONUNCIATION	word stress
SPEAKING	giving instructions

How can playing games be good for you?

A. Discuss these questions with your classmates.

1. "Playing games is a waste of time." Do you agree with this statement? Why or why not?

2. What games did you play as child? Do you ever play games now? If so, which ones?

3. Look at the photo. What kind of game are the women playing?

B. Listen to *The Q Classroom* online. Then answer these questions.

1. What good things do Yuna and Marcus say about games like soccer and chess?

[handwritten: soccer, work team, fix, charaving, give life lesson, share together to win, work together to win]

2. What does Felix say about how games can help us? *[handwritten: relax]*

3. Why does Sophy think that games are a good social activity?

[handwritten: fun together to build relashionship]

iQ PRACTICE Go to the online discussion board to discuss the Unit Question with your classmates. *Practice > Unit 6 > Activity 1*

[handwritten: pull, tug, optimisim, possitive, Pessimism, negative]

UNIT OBJECTIVE ▶ Listen to a talk and a news report. Gather information and ideas to develop and present an educational game.

It is important to review your notes as soon as possible after taking them. When you take notes, you write only single words and short phrases. If you wait too long, you might forget what these mean or why they are important. As you review your notes, edit them and add more information. Your notes will then be a more useful tool for studying. Note: It is a good idea to leave space on the page when you take notes, so you can add more information later.

A. INVESTIGATE Listen to a short talk about the board game Monopoly. Then review one student's notes. Fill in the blanks and add other information you remember.

Monopoly

Monopoly

A. About game

   3rd most pop. game   in world

   about buy and sell propertyis

   players pay rent when   they use some one property

   Goal = win most have money

B. History

   Invent Charles Darrow 19 33

   Darrow got idea earlier game: land road   that   was

   invented   by   actves   Lizzie Magie 1903

   Different rules: player can choose   pay some rent to

   Public Treasury

   All players got share of the money

C. Conclusion   Many poor people Then the Time

   so she wanted to know our society

Lizzie Magie's Landlord

Can chose to pay part of vent Into public tosure

B. ANALYZE Compare your notes with a partner. Listen again, if necessary.

iQ PRACTICE Go online for more practice with reviewing and editing notes.
Practice > Unit 6 > Activity 2

Dates and other numbers are often important details when you are listening, whether a friend is telling a story or you're listening to a news report or a lecture.

Pay attention to numbers and dates as you listen. If possible, write them down with brief notes to remind yourself why they are important.

A. APPLY Look at the dates and numbers in the box. Listen to the short talk about the word game Scrabble™. Then complete each sentence with the correct information.

| 1948 | 1938 | 1952 | 1991 | 4 | 25 | 100 |

1. Alfred Mosher Butts invented the game of Scrabble in ___1938___ .

2. In ___1948___, Butts and his partner, James Brunot, started a Scrabble factory.

3. Between ___1952___ and 2000, people bought more than ___100___ million Scrabble games.

4. One out of every ___4___ families in the United States has a Scrabble game in their home.

5. Scrabble is played in more than ___25___ languages around the world.

6. The first World Scrabble Championship was in ___1919___ .

Scrabble™

B. EXTEND Work with a partner. Practice listening for dates and numbers.

1. Write two original sentences about any topic, each one with a year and another number.

Example: In 2017, there were 3,500 students in my university.

a. ___In 2022, I bought a house with 1 million.___

b. ___In 2022, I spend $2000 for clothing a month.___

2. Read your sentences to a partner and listen to your partner's sentences. Say the dates and numbers you hear.

iQ PRACTICE Go online for more practice with listening for dates and other numbers. *Practice > Unit 6 > Activity 3*

(handwritten, left margin:) In 2022, I boonated 100 $ to save world

(faint handwriting, bottom:) In 2022, I came to the US to study ... for 364 days and now I found that how difficot live in the world.

LISTENING 1

Why Should Adults Play Video Games?

OBJECTIVE ▶

You are going to listen to a game developer give an informal talk about the benefits of video games for adults. As you listen, gather information and ideas about how playing games can be good for you.

VOCABULARY SKILL REVIEW

In Unit 5, you learned about word families. Look at the underlined words in Activity A. Can you find other word forms for them? Use a dictionary if needed.

PREVIEW THE LISTENING

A. VOCABULARY Here are some words from Listening 1. Read the sentences. Then choose the answer that best matches the meaning of each <u>underlined</u> word.

1. A game <u>developer</u> needs to have a lot of fresh, new ideas for games. He or she must be a good computer programmer.

   a. person who makes things   *developer*

   b. person who sells things

2. Before deciding which sport to practice, you need to consider the <u>benefits</u> of each one.

   a. prices

   b. good points   *benefit*

3. These days, it is possible to have many forms of <u>entertainment</u>, such as games and music, in your own home.

   a. things that are fun and interesting   *entertaiment*

   b. things that help people work

4. That math program has had a _positive_ effect on my son. He's beginning to understand algebra very well. (adj)

    a. good   positive

    b. bad

5. The _object_ of the game of Scrabble is to win the most points with the words you make. (n)

    a. place

    b. goal   object

6. You've been under a lot of _stress_ lately. Let's play a game! It'll help you feel better. (n)

    a. state of worry   stress

    b. state of being happy

7. Knowing how to speak in public is a _useful_ skill. Sometimes you will have to make a presentation at work. (adj)

    a. not making a mistake

    b. helpful for doing something   useful

8. You never know how someone will _react_ when they lose a game. (v)

    a. do or say something because of something else that happened   react

    b. tell a lot of people about something that happened

iQ PRACTICE Go online for more practice with the vocabulary.
Practice › Unit 6 › Activities 4–5

ACADEMIC LANGUAGE
The word _benefit_ is often used in academic speaking and writing. It can be used to draw attention to a point to consider. _Consider the benefits of decreasing stress by the simple act of playing video games._

⎯⎯⎯⎯⎯ **OPAL**
Oxford Phrasal Academic Lexicon

B. PREVIEW You are going to listen to a game developer talk about video games. Who do you think plays video games more, children or adults? Why?

WORK WITH THE LISTENING

TIP FOR SUCCESS

When listening to a talk or lecture, sit slightly forward in your seat. This position will help you concentrate, and you will understand more.

A. IDENTIFY Listen to a talk about the benefits of playing video games. The speaker will mention four benefits. Number the pictures in the order you hear them.

Reduce stress

Improve hand-eye coordination

Use as a learning tool

Practice skills useful in the workplace

bad
too much

iQ RESOURCES Go online to download extra vocabulary support.
Resources > Extra Vocabulary > Unit 6

B. LISTEN AND TAKE NOTES Prepare the chart for taking notes. Write the four benefits from Activity A. Then listen again and take notes on the examples the speaker uses to illustrate each benefit.

	Benefits	Examples
1	help eye cordination	svign play game
2	practice skill work place	make creation develop stragty
3	gret Toll leaning	
4	reduce stres diffrence stres from life	reduce real life stres

react quickly
save plane
feel good
history math

C. APPLY Listen again. Complete the sentences with the missing information.

1. In 2018, ___72___ percent of video gamers were over 18 years of age.

2. Of these, ___43___ percent were ___25___ years of age or older.

3. Surgeons who played video games at least __3__ hours per week made __32__ percent fewer mistakes.

4. More than __72__ percent of students who played educational games felt that the games helped them understand subjects like history and math.

D. CATEGORIZE Read the statements. Write *T* (true) or *F* (false). Then work with a partner to correct the false statements.

__T__ 1. The speaker admits that there can be problems with playing video games too often.

__F__ 2. Games about historical events cannot be both entertaining and educational.

__F__ 3. The speaker says that skills used in video games are not useful at work.

__F__ 4. Playing fast-action games is very exciting but also creates stress.

__T__ 5. Video games can have positive effects on a player's feelings.

__T__ 6. The speaker thinks parents should play video games with their children.

E. EXPLAIN Work with a partner. Ask and answer the questions. Give examples and explanations as you discuss each question.

1. How do video games improve hand-eye coordination?

2. How can video games help students study subjects like math and history?

3. What features of video games may help users relax and reduce stress?

iQ PRACTICE Go online for additional listening and comprehension.
Practice ▸ Unit 6 ▸ Activity 6

SAY WHAT YOU THINK

DISCUSS Discuss the questions in a small group.

1. In the listening, the speaker reported that more adults play video games than children. Did this fact surprise you? Why or why not?

2. Do you think that playing video games is an appropriate activity for an adult? Why or why not?

3. The speaker mentions that video gamers may spend too much time playing games. What other problems might people have with playing video games?

Chess Champions

You are going to listen to a news report about children who play chess. As you listen, gather information and ideas about how playing games can be good for you.

PREVIEW THE LISTENING

A. VOCABULARY Here are some words from Listening 2. Read the definitions. Then complete each sentence with the correct word.

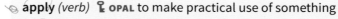

> **apply** *(verb)* 🍴 OPAL to make practical use of something
> **coach** *(noun)* 🍴 a person who trains people to compete in a sport or game
> **competitive** *(adjective)* 🍴 eager to win or be more successful than others
> **disappointment** *(noun)* the state of being disappointed, sad because you did not succeed at something
> **lose** *(verb)* 🍴 to not win; to be defeated in a game
> **pressure** *(noun)* 🍴 OPAL an unhappy feeling caused by the need to succeed or to behave in a particular way
> **tournament** *(noun)* a competition in which many players or teams play against each other
> **wonderful** *(adjective)* 🍴 very good; giving great pleasure

🍴 Oxford 3000™ words   **OPAL** Oxford Phrasal Academic Lexicon

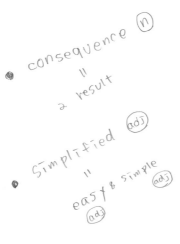

consequence (n)
 =
 a result

Simplified (adj)
 =
 easy & simple (adj)
 (adj)

associate
 =
 relate, connect

compete ✓

1. That player is too __competitive__. He wants to win every game and feels angry when he doesn't.

2. The __coach__ taught the team the rules of the game and helped them develop good strategies.

3. If the children __apply__ his ideas, they will be better players.

4. It's a big __disappointment__ when you don't win, but you can learn a lot from losing.

5. Our club is going to play in an important chess __tournament__ next month. Teams from all over the city will be there.

6. Your team won all your games. Congratulations! That's __wonderful__!

7. In chess, even if you think that you do everything right, you can still __lose__ the game.

8. Parents shouldn't put a lot of __pressure__ on their children by telling them they have to win every game.

iQ PRACTICE Go online for more practice with the vocabulary.
Practice > Unit 6 > Activities 7–8

engage ⓥ   to interest or attract someone to something

evaluate = assess ⓥ   to judge or form an oppinion about something

like affect ⓥ impact ⓝ   An affect or impression made on something or someone

to act = simulate ⓥ   to imitate the appearance or character of something
(simjəleIt)   *simulate*

Power plant ⓝ   A place where electricity is generated

zone ⓝ   A area with paticular use

B. PREVIEW You are going to listen to a news report about children who play chess. Work with a partner. Answer the questions.

1. What do you know about the game of chess? Discuss.

2. Work with your partner to identify the chess pieces in the pictures. Write the correct name under each picture.

king   queen   knight   bishop

a. _____King_____

b. _____Queen_____

c. _____Bishop_____

d. _____Knight_____

3. How can children benefit from playing a game like chess?

WORK WITH THE LISTENING

A. INVESTIGATE Listen to the news report. Don't take notes. Work with a partner to discuss what you each remember hearing.

B. LISTEN AND TAKE NOTES Listen to the news report again. Take notes using the headings in the chart.

More children playing chess	

Benefits of playing chess	✓ usufull skills ✓ lean head ✓ learn real life ✓ take time to think
Does chess cause stress?	
What to do when children lose a game	⊖ Don't angree ⊖ Do not put too much stress

⊕ tell them best play

C. IDENTIFY Read the questions. Choose the correct answers. Use your notes to help you.

1. When do some schools now offer chess clubs and classes?

   a. only in high school

   ✓ b. starting in kindergarten

   c. starting in the fourth grade

2. Who did the Panda Pawns compete against in their chess tournament?

   a. college students

   b. elementary school students

   ✓ c. high school students

3. How did the young player named Lauren say that chess helped her?

   a. It helped her learn the different moves in the game.

   ✓ b. It helped her learn to think ahead in real-life situations.

   c. It helped her make new friends with other chess players.

4. What did the coach say he liked about chess?

   ✓ a. Players have to take time to think.

   b. It's a fast game and players have to think fast.

   c. Technology is making it a better game.

5. What did Dr. Ochoa think about the children's experience at the tournaments?

√ a. They were excited and seemed to have a wonderful time.

   b. The competition put them under too much stress.

   c. Their teachers made them feel that winning was very important.

6. Which statement would Dr. Ochoa probably NOT agree with?

   a. Playing chess should be fun for children.

   b. Playing chess will help children later in their lives.

   c. Playing chess causes too much stress when a child loses.

 ## CRITICAL THINKING STRATEGY

Identifying "false" inferences

An **inference** is a logical conclusion. It is an idea that you decide is probably true based on the information you have. It is reasonable and makes good sense. In this example, the information strongly supports the conclusion, or inference. Note that the inference is probable, or likely, but not certain.

Information	Inference
Jacob has just finished playing a chess game. He doesn't look very happy.	He probably lost the game.

Sometimes people make "false" inferences. In these cases, there is not enough information to support the conclusion.

Information	False inference
An eight-year-old boy from Nigeria won a New York State chess tournament.	People from Nigeria are great chess players.

The fact that one person, or even many people, from a country are good at something does not mean that everyone is.

iQ PRACTICE Go online to watch the Critical Thinking Video and check your comprehension. *Practice > Unit 6 > Activity 9*

D. ANALYZE Read the sentences. Check the correct box for each sentence: "Supported inference" or "False inference" based on the news report. Hint: There are two of each.

	Supported inference	False inference
1. Many schools believe that playing chess is good for their students.	☐	☐
2. Dr. Ochoa thinks all schools should have chess clubs like the Panda Pawns.	☐	☐
3. Many parents get angry when their child loses a game.	☐	☐
4. Losing a game can be a good learning experience.	☐	☐

E. EXPLAIN Compare answers with a partner. Explain why each answer is either a supported inference or a false one.

WORK WITH THE VIDEO

A. PREVIEW Do you think playing video games in school could help students learn? How?

VIDEO VOCABULARY

engage (v.) to interest or attract someone to something

assess (v.) to judge or form an opinion about something

impact (n.) an effect or impression made on someone or something

simulate (v.) to imitate the appearance or character of something

power plant (n.) a place where electricity is generated

zone (n.) an area with a particular use, for example, for homes or businesses

iQ RESOURCES Go online to watch the video about using video games in the classroom. *Resources > Video > Unit 6 > Unit Video*

B. CATEGORIZE Watch the video two or three times. Read the statements. Write *T* (true) or *F* (false).

_____ 1. Jessica Lindl, the narrator in the video, says that bringing video games into the classroom will help prepare students for success in the 21st century.

_____ 2. Lindl thinks the education system has already changed and is taking advantage of new technology.

_____ 3. She thinks that since playing video games has become so common, it's easier for people to imagine using games in the classroom.

_____ 4. In the video game called SimCity, students solve real-world problems in a simulated city.

_____ 5. Lindl says that moving from one level to another in a video game by learning certain skills is similar to taking tests to make progress in school.

_____ 6. In the example Lindl gives about SimCity, a city has a major problem with its water supply.

_____ 7. Many kids playing SimCity tried to solve the problem by turning off all the power plants. That was the correct decision.

_____ 8. Lindl thinks that most schools are preparing students for success by using new technology and innovations.

C. EXTEND Jessica Lindl believes that bringing video games into the classroom will help prepare students for life in the 21st century. Do you agree or disagree with this idea? Why?

SAY WHAT YOU THINK

SYNTHESIZE Think about the unit video, Listening 1, and Listening 2 as you discuss the questions.

1. Think about games or sports you play frequently. What can you learn from playing them? How can they make learning easier?

2. Listening 1 and Listening 2 mention games as a form of entertainment, as something "fun." How important is fun in our lives?

3. Do you agree with the following statement? Why or why not?

   "We don't stop playing because we grow old; we grow old because we stop playing."
   – George Bernard Shaw (playwright, 1856–1950)

VOCABULARY SKILL Word families: suffixes

A **suffix** is a word or syllable placed after a root word. A suffix often changes the part of speech of the word. For example, the suffixes *-ion* or *-tion* often mark the change from a verb to a noun. Adding the suffix sometimes results in other spelling changes. Here are some examples.

verb	noun
compete	competi**tion**
produce	produc**tion**
react	reac**tion**

A. APPLY Complete the chart with the noun form of each verb. Use the suffixes *-ion* or *-tion*. Use a dictionary to check for possible spelling changes.

Verb	Noun
coordinate	coordination
discuss	discussion
inform	information
instruct	instruction
operate	operation
pronounce	pronunciation (prəninsТéiʃən)

B. APPLY Complete each sentence with the noun form of the verb in parentheses. Use a dictionary to check spelling if necessary.

1. The __presentation__ (present) of the prizes will take place on the last day of the competition.

2. The teacher will make the __introduction__ (introduce), and then the winners will speak.

3. Who made the __decision__ (decide) to start a chess club?

4. More than one person worked to develop the game. It was a __creation__ (create) based on the work of many departments.

5. Thomas Edison had little formal __education__ (educate). His mother taught him at home.

iQ PRACTICE Go online for more practice with suffixes.
Practice > Unit 6 > Activity 10

noun

ation

nce

steriliz (v)

sterilization (n)

optimize (v)

optimization (n)

用来适应于多

OBJECTIVE ▶   At the end of this unit, you are going to work in a group to develop an educational game. As part of the game development, you will have to give instructions to the players.

GRAMMAR   Imperative verbs

Kind of Command

Use affirmative and negative **imperatives** to give instructions and directions.

For affirmative imperatives, use **the base form of the verb**.

> **Raise** your hands.
> **Look** at the people around you.

For negative imperatives, use **do not** or **don't** + **the base form of the verb**. *Don't* is more common when speaking. Using *do not* when speaking can make the imperative sound stronger.

> **Don't spend** too much time playing games.
> **Do not move** your queen there!

In imperative sentences, *you* is "understood" as the subject of the verb. We don't usually say or write the word *you*. However, when you are giving a long list of instructions, using *you* from time to time sounds more polite.

> Next, **you** move the queen out to attack.

iQ RESOURCES   **Go online to watch the Grammar Skill Video.**
Resources > Video > Unit 6 > Grammar Skill Video

A. APPLY Complete the conversation. Use the imperative phrases in the box. Then practice the conversation with a partner.

do *not* tell	don't say	put up one finger
take one	use your hands	you act out

Khalid: We're playing charades. Do you want to play?

Max: Charades? What's that? I've never heard of it.

Khalid: It's a game. You act out things, and the other players have to guess them. We're acting out common activities.

Max: Sounds interesting. I'd like to try it.

Khalid: Good. Just do as I say. First, ____take one____ of

the cards from this box and read it silently. ____do not tell____

anyone what it says.

Max: OK. I did that. And now?

Khalid: Now, you are on our team. Next, _____
                                                          3

what it says. _____ and your body, but
                                4

_____ anything. Then we try to guess what it is.
            5

Max: You mean I can't talk at all?

Khalid: That's right. There are things you can do for some common words. For

example, _____ for the number one, two for two,
                            6

etc. Make a *T* with your fingers and it means the word *the*.

Max: OK. Here goes. I'll give it a try.

Khalid: You're driving a car!

Max: That's right. Hey, that was easy. Khalid, now it's your turn.

🔊 **B. EVALUATE** Listen and check your answers.

C. CREATE Work with a partner. Tell your partner how to do something. Use imperative verbs. Choose one of the topics below or use your own idea.

- How to send an email
- How to learn a new word
- How to remember people's names
- How to lose a game politely

iQ PRACTICE Go online for more practice with imperative verbs.
Practice > Unit 6 > Activity 11

iQ PRACTICE Go online for the Grammar Expansion: imperative sentences.
Practice > Unit 6 > Activity 12

PRONUNCIATION Word stress

When learning the pronunciation of a word, it is important to know which syllable to stress. If you put the stress on the wrong syllable, the listener might not understand it. The position of the stressed syllable varies in words with three or more syllables.

Notice where the main stress falls in these words.

1st syllable	2nd syllable	3rd syllable
be-ne-fit	im-**por**-tance	en-ter-**tain**-ment

There are some patterns that can help you decide which syllable to stress. For example, words ending with the suffix *–tion* stress the syllable before the suffix.

ed-u-**ca**-tion   com-pe-**ti**-tion

Sometimes you have to look up a word in the dictionary or ask someone to say the word for you to learn the correct pronunciation. When English speakers see a word they don't know, they often ask, "How do you pronounce this word?"

 A. IDENTIFY Listen to the words. Underline the stressed syllable.

TIP FOR SUCCESS

Learning the correct pronunciation of a long word helps you remember the word. Then you will say it with the same stress and rhythm every time you use it.

Words with 3 syllables	Words with 4 syllables	Word with 5+ syllables
intro<u>duce</u>	competitive	elementary
excited	experience	coordination
messages	understanding	creativity

B. APPLY Listen to the words and repeat. Focus on using the correct stress.

1. positive
2. situation
3. wonderful
4. disappointment
5. organizers
6. tournament
7. developer
8. destruction

iQ PRACTICE Go online for more practice with word stress.
Practice › Unit 6 › Activity 13

SPEAKING SKILL Giving instructions

When you are giving **instructions** about how to do something, first give a general description of the task. For example, to tell someone how to play a game, give some general information about the game and tell them what the object of the game is. Then present the steps in the correct order. Use phrases like these to make your instructions clear.

┌ **The object of the game is to** score the most points.
└ **Here's how to** act out the words in charades.

Use order words and phrases to make the sequence of the steps clear.

┌ **First**, take one of the cards from the box.
 Next, you have to act out what it says.
 After that, the other team takes a turn.
└ **Finally**, the team with the most correct guesses wins the game.

A. APPLY Listen to the conversation about bowling. Complete the conversation with the words and phrases that make the instructions clear. Then practice the conversation with a partner.

Mi-rae: Is this your first time bowling? Don't worry. I can tell you how the game works.

Liana: OK. What do we do?

Mi-rae: Do you see those white things? They're called pins. The _____ of the game is to knock them down with a ball. You roll the
₁

Bowling   ball down the lane to hit them.

Liana: That sounds easy. What do I do first?

Mi-rae: _____ , choose a ball. Pick one that isn't too heavy
₂
for you.

Liana: OK. I think I'm going to use this ball. I really like the color. What do I do

_____ ?
     3

Mi-rae: _____ , you hold the ball with your fingers in the holes.
           4

_____ , you stand in front of the lane. Do you understand so far?
     5

Liana: Yes. I get it so far. _____ what do I do? Do I roll it with both
                 6

hands?

Mi-rae: No, the _____ is to roll it with one hand.
             7

_____ , try to roll it down the middle of the lane.
     8

Liana: OK. Wow! I knocked down all the pins!

Mi-rae: Great! That's called a strike. You're going to be good at bowling!

B. IDENTIFY Read the instructions about how to play hide and seek. Put the instructions in the correct order. Write 1 to 5 next to the sentences.

____ Then, the other players hide while the seeker counts.

____ Finally, players try to return to the base. A player who is tagged, or touched, by the seeker loses.

____ Second, the seeker stands at the base, closes his or her eyes, and counts to 20.

_1_ First, choose one player in the group to seek, or look for, the other players.

____ Next, the seeker tries to find the hidden players.

iQ PRACTICE Go online for more practice with giving instructions.
Practice > Unit 6 > Activity 14

Hide and seek

TIP FOR SUCCESS

Stop from time to time and check that listeners understand your instructions. Ask a specific question or say something like, "Are you with me so far?"

UNIT ASSIGNMENT Develop and present an idea for a new game

OBJECTIVE ▶

In this section, you are going to work in a group to develop an educational game that can help people in their real lives. It can be any kind of game: a video game, a board game, etc. You will then present it to the class. As you prepare your game, think about the Unit Question, "How can playing games be good for you?" Use information from Listening 1, Listening 2, the unit video, and your work in this unit to support your presentation. Refer to the Self-Assessment checklist on page 136.

CONSIDER THE IDEAS

A. INVESTIGATE Read these tips about developing games.

Home		Q	Sign in 👤

Game Development – How to get started!

To develop a game, it's a good idea to work with two or three other people. A group creates more ideas, and you can test the game to see how it's working. Here are a few tips to help you get started.

- First, think of a theme (main topic) for your game. It's usually more interesting if it's about some real-life situation such as work, travel, or family life.

- Next, narrow the topic so that it is something that is easily understood by the game players.

- Decide what kind of game it will be—a video game, a traditional board game, or perhaps a game that doesn't need any equipment, like charades.

- Decide what the goal of the game is. How do players move? How does someone win the game? Is it a video game with a story?

- Write a short list of possible rules. How does the game start? What do players do during the game? Is there anything players cannot do?

- List objects people will need to play the game. If possible, make some drawings to show what the game will look like.

- Test the game. Make sure that it is easy to play. Have other people test it, too.

The most important thing is to make sure the game is fun and easy to learn. Players should be able to learn something as they play.

B. DISCUSS Work in a group. Answer the questions.

1. Why is it better to work with a group to develop a game?

2. What kind of themes do the tips on page 134 suggest?

3. What are some of the most important things to do when you develop a game?

PREPARE AND SPEAK

A. GATHER IDEAS Work in a group. Agree on a theme for your game and decide what type of game it will be. Use an idea from the list below or think of your own idea.

- a game that helps people learn English
- a game that helps students learn about a kind of math
- a game about visiting other countries

B. ORGANIZE IDEAS With your group, develop a plan for your game. Use the tips on page 134. Follow these steps.

1. Discuss and plan the game. Remember to keep the game very simple.

2. Create a list of rules and collect the materials you need.

3. Prepare drawings or other items that will help with your presentation.

4. Practice the presentation. Make sure that everyone in the group has a part. The presentation should include these points:

   - The name and object of the game

   - The steps followed to play the game

   - Any special rules players need to know

   - An explanation of how the game ends

   - What players can learn by playing the game

C. SPEAK Give your presentation to the class or to another group. Refer to the Self-Assessment checklist on page 136 before you begin.

iQ PRACTICE Go online for your alternate Unit Assignment.
Practice > Unit 6 > Activity 15

CHECK AND REFLECT

A. CHECK Think about the Unit Assignment as you complete the Self-Assessment checklist.

SELF-ASSESSMENT	Yes	No
I was able to speak easily about the topic.	☐	☐
The class or my group understood me.	☐	☐
I used imperative verbs.	☐	☐
I used vocabulary from the unit.	☐	☐
I gave instructions.	☐	☐
I used correct word stress.	☐	☐

B. REFLECT Discuss these questions with a partner or group.

1. What is something new you learned in this unit?

2. Look back at the Unit Question—How can playing games be good for you? Is your answer different now than when you started the unit? If yes, how is it different? Why?

iQ PRACTICE Go to the online discussion board to discuss the questions. *Practice > Unit 6 > Activity 16*

TRACK YOUR SUCCESS

iQ PRACTICE Go online to check the words and phrases you have learned in this unit. *Practice > Unit 6 > Activity 17*

Check (✓) the skills and strategies you learned. If you need more work on a skill, refer to the page(s) in parentheses.

NOTE-TAKING	☐ I can review and edit my notes. (p. 114)
LISTENING	☐ I can recognize dates and other numbers. (p. 115)
CRITICAL THINKING	☐ I can identify "false" inferences. (p. 124)
VOCABULARY	☐ I can recognize suffixes in word families. (p. 127)
GRAMMAR	☐ I can recognize and use imperative verbs. (p. 129)
PRONUNCIATION	☐ I can use correct word stress. (p. 131)
SPEAKING	☐ I can give clear instructions. (p. 132)
OBJECTIVE ▶	☐ I can gather information and ideas to develop and present an educational game.

Environmental Science

NOTE-TAKING	preparing to take notes in class
CRITICAL THINKING	categorizing
LISTENING	recognizing a speaker's attitude
VOCABULARY	compound nouns
GRAMMAR	future with *will*
PRONUNCIATION	word stress in compound nouns
SPEAKING	summarizing

How do people survive in extreme environments?

A. Discuss these questions with your classmates.

1. What do you think the term *extreme environment* means? Give examples.

2. Do you think you could survive in one of these extreme environments? Why or why not?

3. Look at the picture. Do you think many people live here? Why or why not?

B. Listen to *The Q Classroom* online. Then answer these questions.

1. What examples does Yuna give of extreme environments?

2. What example does Felix give?

3. How does Sophy explain Felix's example?

4. What possible extreme environment does Marcus talk about?

iQ PRACTICE Go to the online discussion board to discuss the Unit Question with your classmates. *Practice > Unit 7 > Activity 1*

UNIT OBJECTIVE

Watch a video and listen to a follow-up discussion. Then listen to a news report. Gather information and ideas to role-play an interview about surviving in an extreme environment.

NOTE-TAKING SKILL Preparing to take notes in class

Before you go to a class, make sure you read all the assignments. They will often contain key words and ideas that the instructor will use in the classroom. As you read, write down these key words and ideas. Look up unfamiliar words to check their meaning and pronunciation. Pronunciation is important because it is sometimes difficult to recognize a word when you hear it in context, even if you know the word.

Use your "pre-class" notes in the classroom. Listen for the key words and add more information to your notes.

VOCABULARY SKILL REVIEW

In Unit 6, you learned about two common English suffixes that change a verb to a noun. Notice here that the suffix *-ic* changes the noun *nomad* to the adjective *nomadic*. What other suffixes can you identify in this introduction?

A. IDENTIFY Read the introduction to a video titled *The Nomads of Outer Mongolia* about a nomadic people known as the Darhad. Prepare notes and look up words you don't know in a dictionary. Check both meaning and pronunciation.

Outer Mongolia. Just hearing this name brings to mind a place that is far, far away. Mongolia is indeed a very remote country. It lies between China to the south and the Russian province of Siberia to the north. It is a landlocked country, which means that it is completely surrounded by land and has no coastline. It is also a country of extremes. Temperatures can fall to –40 degrees Celsius in the winter in the north and be as high as 40 degrees Celsius in the Gobi Desert in the southern part of the country.

Mongolia is a large country geographically—nineteenth in the world— with a small population of just over three million people. Because very little of the country is suitable for agriculture, raising animals is an important part of the economy. People raise sheep and cattle, as well as goats, horses, and camels. About 30 percent of the population, including the Darhad, still lead a traditional nomadic lifestyle. This means that during the year they move from place to place as they look for good pasture for their animals. They live in round, tent-like structures called *gers* or *yurts* that they can take down and carry with them from place to place.

B. EXPLAIN What words did you look up? Compare with a partner.

Sheep and goats in a pasture

iQ PRACTICE Go online for more practice with preparing to take notes in class. *Practice ▶ Unit 7 ▶ Activity 2*

LISTENING 1

OBJECTIVE ▶

The Nomads of Outer Mongolia

You are going to watch a video about the Darhad people. Then you will listen to a class discussion about it. As you watch and listen, gather information and ideas about how people survive in extreme environments.

A Mongolian yurt, or *ger*

PREVIEW THE LISTENING

A. VOCABULARY Here are some words from Listening 1. Read the definitions. Then complete each sentence with the correct word.

attack *(verb)* 🔑 OPAL to try to hurt or defeat someone by using force

fascinating *(adjective)* 🔑 extremely interesting

freezing *(adjective)* 🔑 very cold; the temperature at which water becomes ice, or freezes

permanent *(adjective)* 🔑 lasting a long time or forever; that will not change

process *(verb)* 🔑 OPAL to treat something (for example, with chemicals) in order to change it

remain *(verb)* 🔑 to be left after other people or things have gone

suitable *(adjective)* 🔑 OPAL right or convenient for someone or something

threat *(noun)* 🔑 OPAL a person or thing that may damage something or hurt someone

🔑 Oxford 3000™ words   **OPAL** Oxford Phrasal Academic Lexicon

1. There are a lot of trees around our house. When the weather is very dry, fire is a serious _____.

2. I'm going to a formal dinner. Is this green jacket _____? Maybe I should wear the black one and wear a tie.

3. We've lived here for 20 years, and we're not planning to move. It's our _____ home.

4. They will _____ in Florida until the winter is over and then come home.

5. We're expecting _____ weather tonight. I'm sure there will be ice on the lake in the morning!

6. If you think a wolf is going to _____ you, don't run. Shout and make yourself look scary.

7. We've just seen a _____ program about the Inuit people of northern Alaska. What an interesting way of life!

8. Over there, the workers _____ the cream and milk in order to make butter and ice cream.

iQ PRACTICE Go online for more practice with the vocabulary.
Practice ⟩ Unit 7 ⟩ Activities 3–4

B. **PREVIEW** You are going to watch the video *The Nomads of Outer Mongolia* and listen to a class discussion about it. What do you think is extreme about the environment in which the Darhad people live? Discuss this question with a partner. Give examples.

WORK WITH THE LISTENING

iQ RESOURCES Go online to watch the video.
Resources ⟩ Video ⟩ Unit 7 ⟩ Listening 1 Part 1

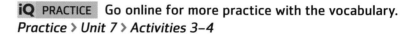

A. **LISTEN AND TAKE NOTES** Review your "pre-class" notes from Activity A on page 140. Then takes notes as you watch the video* and listen to the discussion.

iQ RESOURCES Go online to download extra vocabulary support.
Resources ⟩ Extra Vocabulary ⟩ Unit 7

TIP FOR SUCCESS
When possible, watch movies or videos with English captions. This will improve your listening skills as you hear the words and read them at the same time. It is an enjoyable way to practice listening.

*Audio version available. *Resources ⟩ Audio ⟩ Unit 7*

B. ANALYZE How did the Note-taking activity help you when you were taking notes?

C. IDENTIFY Read the sentences. Choose the answer that best completes each statement. Use your notes to help you.

1. Nomads are people who ____.

    a. live in one place all their lives

    b. travel from one place to another during the year

    c. make almost everything they need themselves

2. The Darhad people use their animals mostly ____.

    a. for food and clothing

    b. as protection from wolves

    c. to help them move around

3. The Darhad live in ____.

    a. small houses

    b. wooden buildings

    c. felt-lined tents

4. One danger the Darhad face is ____.

    a. traveling over the mountains

    b. herding their animals

    c. being attacked by wolves

5. The Darhad people move from place to place because ____.

    a. their animals need good places to find food

    b. it isn't safe for them to stay in one place

    c. they need to buy things from traders

6. The Darhad ____ in order to buy things from traders.

    a. have to use cash

    b. can use things they make such as cheese

    c. have to travel to the city

7. Felt is a material that the Darhad use ____.

    a. to make their tents

    b. as a food for their animals

    c. when they buy things from traders

D. EXPLAIN Match each statement with a supporting idea given by one of the speakers. Listen to the discussion again to check your answers.

____ 1. Traders are also nomads in some ways.

____ 2. The Darhad's lifestyle seems like a healthy one.

____ 3. It's important for the Darhad to keep their traditional lifestyle.

____ 4. Many nomads are leaving and going to the cities.

____ 5. The nomadic life is very hard.

____ 6. The students would not be able to live like the Darhad people.

   a. They think they will have a better life there.

   b. They live close to nature and in a close community.

   c. They travel around and sell things to the nomads.

   d. They shouldn't let modern society change their customs.

   e. The Darhad people know how to survive in an extreme environment.

   f. They climb mountains in the winter when it is minus 40 degrees.

CRITICAL THINKING STRATEGY

Categorizing

When we **categorize** information, we separate items into groups according to certain criteria or characteristics. When categorizing, first decide what these criteria or characteristics will be. For example, a collection of books can be grouped by topic: fiction, history, science, etc. Or you could group them by author, or even by the colors of the covers for a decorative effect. It all depends on your reasons for categorizing.

iQ PRACTICE Go online to watch the Critical Thinking Video and check your comprehension. *Practice > Unit 7 > Activity 5*

E. CATEGORIZE The words in the list represent important parts of the Darhad people's lives. Write each word in the appropriate category in the chart.

camels	cheese	freezing	goats	milk
mountains	pastures	sheep	snow	tents
valleys	winter	wolves	yogurt	

Animals	Features of the land	Weather	Food and supplies

F. EXPLAIN Work with a partner. Say why each of the items in Activity F is important to the Darhad people.

iQ PRACTICE Go online for additional listening and comprehension.
Practice > Unit 7 > Activity 6

SAY WHAT YOU THINK

DISCUSS Discuss the questions in a small group.

1. What do you think is the most interesting thing about the Darhad way of life? Why?

2. Do you think you could survive life with the Darhad community? Why or why not?

3. Ellen thinks it is important for people like the Darhad to keep their traditional lifestyle. Jon thinks this is not realistic because many nomads are leaving to go live in the cities. Who do you agree with more, Ellen or Jon? Why?

LISTENING SKILL Recognizing a speaker's attitude

Speakers communicate **attitudes** and feelings through tone of voice as well as the words they use. The tone of voice can tell the listener if the speaker is serious or joking. It shows the speaker's feelings about the subject of a conversation—positive or negative.

If you can see the speaker, his or her body language and facial expressions can tell you a lot about the speaker's attitude. If you can't see the speaker, you have to guess the speaker's attitude from the tone of his or her voice.

A. ANALYZE Listen to part of the conversation again. What does each speaker's voice tell you about his or her attitude or feelings? Discuss the questions.

1. How does Ellen sound when Norah says she would like to live like the Darhad? That is, does Ellen sound angry, surprised, or confused?

2. How do you think Norah feels at first about Ellen's response? For example, is she happy, angry, or sad?

B. INTERPRET Listen to another conversation between Norah, Jon, and Ellen. Work with a partner. Ask and answer the questions.

TIP FOR SUCCESS

Different cultures and languages express attitudes and emotions differently when speaking. It takes time and experience to listen for and understand people's feelings.

1. How does Ellen sound when she first learns that Norah is going to Mongolia—surprised or angry?

2. What does Ellen say to Norah?

3. How does Norah feel about what Ellen says—surprised or angry?

4. Do you think Ellen was rude? Why or why not?

5. How do Ellen and Norah feel at the end of the conversation? Are they angry or happy? How do you know?

iQ PRACTICE Go online for more practice recognizing a speaker's attitude. *Practice > Unit 7 > Activity 7*

High-Rise Living

OBJECTIVE ▶ You are going to listen to a news report about people's experiences living in high-rise buildings. As you listen, gather information and ideas about how people survive in extreme environments.

PREVIEW THE LISTENING

A. VOCABULARY Here are some words from Listening 2. Read the sentences. Then write each <u>underlined</u> word next to the correct definition.

1. At the meeting, each <u>resident</u> who lives in the building will have to vote for or against changing the paint colors.

2. Mount Everest is 8,848 meters high. At that <u>height</u>, there isn't enough air for people to breathe easily.

3. I live on the 40th floor of my building. I'm sometimes late for work because I have to wait for the <u>elevator</u> to get down to the first floor.

4. They live in a <u>suburb</u> of Boston, in an area about 30 minutes outside the city.

5. In 1964, the state of Alaska had an <u>earthquake</u> that measured 9.2. Many buildings were destroyed.

6. This is a great <u>neighborhood</u>. There are a lot of good stores and restaurants nearby.

7. They're waiting for Dave's <u>response</u> to the email. They need his answer before they make a decision.

8. I felt the building <u>shake</u> just now. I think that big truck that drove by made it move.

a. _____ (*verb*) to move from side to side or up and down with short, quick movements

b. _____ (*noun*) a particular part of a city or town and the people who live there

c. _____ (*noun*) a person who lives in a place

d. _____ (*noun*) an answer or reaction to something

e. _____ (*noun*) the measurement from the bottom to the top of a person or thing

f. _____ (*noun*) a sudden, violent movement of the earth's surface

g. _____ (*noun*) a machine in a building that is used to carry people or things from one floor to another

h. _____ (*noun*) an area where people live that is outside the central city

iQ PRACTICE Go online for more practice with the vocabulary.
Practice > Unit 7 > Activities 8–9

B. PREVIEW You are going to listen to a news report about people who live in high-rise buildings. What do you think they will say about their experience? Name one thing.

WORK WITH THE LISTENING

 A. LISTEN AND TAKE NOTES Listen to the news report in which four people describe their experiences living in high-rise buildings. Are they mostly positive, negative, or both? On a sheet of paper, prepare a chart like the one below. As you listen, write the name of the city and mark each one as + (positive), – (negative), or *B* (both).

Person	City	Positive or negative	Notes
1.			
2.			
3.			
4.			

B. EXPLAIN Listen again and add information in your Notes column to explain how each person felt about living in a high-rise building.

C. EVALUATE Compare notes with a partner. Add to and edit your notes as needed.

D. EXPLAIN Answer the questions.

1. Why did the man from Singapore have a problem sleeping when he lived in a high-rise building?

_____

2. How did he feel on windy days?

_____

3. What are two things the woman in Toronto can see from her windows?

_____

4. Is her apartment peaceful or noisy? Why?

_____

5. Why did the family in London decide that the high-rise was not suitable for their family? Give one reason.

_____

6. What did they do?

_____

7. How does the woman in San Francisco feel about living in a high-rise building? Why?

_____

8. What does she worry about?

_____

E. CREATE Work in a small group. Follow these instructions.

1. Choose one topic from the list below. If possible, each person should choose a different topic.

   - High-rise living for families with children

   - Advantages of living in a high-rise building

   - Problems with living in a high-rise building

   - Are high-rise buildings safe, yes or no?

2. Tell the group everything you can about your topic. Use your notes to help you. You can also include your own ideas.

 # SAY WHAT YOU THINK

SYNTHESIZE Think about Listening 1 and Listening 2 as you discuss the questions.

1. Which lifestyle was more interesting for you to learn about, the nomadic life of the Darhad or life on a high floor in a high-rise building? Explain.

2. Have you ever lived in a high-rise building? If so, describe your experience. If not, would you like to? Why or why not?

3. What other extreme environments do people live in? What do you know about them?

VOCABULARY SKILL Compound nouns

A **compound noun** is a noun made up of two nouns or a noun and an adjective.

Some compound nouns are written as one word, like *coastline* (*coast* + *line*).

Others are written as two words, like *motion sickness*.

In a compound noun, the first word says something about the second word. A *coastline* is the outline that marks the coast of an area, or the border between the land and the sea. *Motion sickness* is the sick feeling caused by motion, often in a car, boat, or airplane.

A. APPLY Read the sentences. Then complete each compound noun with a word from the box. Use your dictionary to see if the compound noun is written as one word or two words.

TIP FOR SUCCESS
Check your dictionary to learn if a compound noun is written as one or two words.

board	games	house	market
papers	quake	scrapers	style

1. The strongest earth_____ ever recorded occurred in Chile in 1960. It measured 9.5.

2. Last year, we moved from a big city to a small town in the country. We have a very different life_____.

3. Each pet rock came in a card_____ box that looked like a box for carrying a pet.

4. Can you buy organic foods at that super_____?

5. Sometimes people refer to high-rise buildings as sky_____ because it looks as if they are touching the sky.

6. We have a little store_____ where we put things we don't need very often.

7. People still talk about news_____ even though they are reading them online, with no real "paper."

8. Many adults enjoy playing video_____ as much as or more than children do!

B. RESTATE Try to guess the compound nouns for these definitions. Some hints use both words of the compound word. Others don't.

1. A phone that is intelligent: _____ *a smartphone* _____

2. A game in which players throw a ball through a net called a *basket*:

   _____

3. The light that comes from the sun: _____

4. Saturday and Sunday, two days at the end of the week: _____

5. A store where people can buy books: _____

6. What you call your mother's or father's mother: _____

iQ PRACTICE Go online for more practice with compound nouns.
Practice ⟩ Unit 7 ⟩ Activity 10

SPEAKING

OBJECTIVE ▶

At the end of this unit, you are going to work with a partner to role-play an interview about living in an extreme environment. As part of this role-play, you may have to summarize your or your partner's ideas.

GRAMMAR Future with *will*

Use **will + verb** to talk about the future, that is, about things that have not happened yet. Note that the form *will* never changes. It is the same for all persons and in singular and plural.

> One day people **will live** on Mars.
> She **will leave** next week.

Affirmative contraction

I will = I'll, they will = they'll, he will or *she will = he'll / she'll*

> **They'll allow** more people to live in a smaller area.

Negative contraction

will not = won't

> Humans **won't be** able to breathe the air on Mars.

Yes/No **questions and short answers**

will + subject + verb

> **Will you buy** an apartment in that building?
> Yes, I will. / No, I won't.

Information questions

Question word + *will* + subject + verb

> What **will Norah do** when she's with the Darhad people?

iQ RESOURCES Go online to watch the Grammar Skill Video.
Resources > Video > Unit 7 > Grammar Skill Video

A. APPLY Write sentences with *will* or *won't*. Use your own opinions.

1. Humans / travel / to Mars by 2030

_____

2. Cities / build / more skyscrapers

_____

3. The Darhad / continue / to live their traditional lifestyle

_____

4. I probably / visit / Antarctica one day

_____

5. Nomads / have / a better life in cities

_____

6. Most people / be happier / in a high-rise building

_____

B. **EXPLAIN** Work with a partner. Take turns answering and asking the questions with short answers. Use your own ideas.

A: Will you look for more information about the Darhad people?
B: Yes, I will. I'd like to learn more about them.

1. Will you ever travel to Antarctica?

2. Will you rent an apartment in a high-rise building?

3. Will you get motion-sick if you travel by boat?

4. Will you ever live in a place with an extreme environment?

5. Will you ever go mountain climbing?

iQ PRACTICE Go online for more practice with the future with _will_.
Practice > Unit 7 > Activity 11

iQ PRACTICE Go online for the Grammar Expansion: _be going to_ and _will_.
Practice > Unit 7 > Activity 12

PRONUNCIATION Word stress in compound nouns

Compound nouns are pronounced as if they were one word. The **stress** is usually on the first syllable or word.

coastline   earthquake   lifestyle
skyscraper   smartphone   storehouse

A. **APPLY** Listen and practice the pronunciation of these compound nouns.

1. bookstore
2. website
3. coffee cup
4. shoreline
5. newspaper
6. sunlight

A coastline

B. APPLY Work with a partner. Take turns reading these sentences aloud. Focus on the pronunciation of the compound nouns.

1. Mexico has coastlines along the Pacific Ocean and the Gulf of Mexico.

2. We went for a walk in the moonlight.

3. Those new lightbulbs are supposed to last for ten years.

4. Which sport do you prefer to play, basketball or football?

5. I prefer the lifestyle in the city. The country is too quiet for me.

iQ PRACTICE Go online for more practice with word stress in compound nouns. *Practice > Unit 7 > Activity 13*

SPEAKING SKILL Summarizing

To **summarize** means to present the main ideas of something you hear or read, but in a much shorter form, called a *summary*. A good summary:

- is short and clear.

- focuses on the main ideas, not the details.

- gives the speaker's ideas, not your opinions.

When speaking, you can summarize to:

- check your understanding of the main points in a conversation.

- tell someone briefly about something you heard or read.

A. EVALUATE Read the summaries of the video from Listening 1. Check (✓) the best summary. Why is it the best summary? Discuss with a partner.

The Nomads of Outer Mongolia

☐ 1. The video was about a group of nomads who live in Mongolia. They live in tents and have animals. Sometimes they buy things from traders. I don't think I'd like living the way the Darhad people do. For one thing, I really don't like cold weather or climbing mountains.

☐ 2. The video was about the lifestyle of the Darhad people, nomads in Mongolia. They travel from one place to another each year to find food for their animals. Their lives are difficult and full of danger such as attacks by wolves and extremely cold winters.

☐ 3. The video was about the Darhad people, who are nomads. They make most things they need themselves. They make cheese from milk from their animals. Sometimes they buy things from traders. It's very cold where they live.

B. RESTATE Work with a partner. Follow these instructions.

1. Listen to the news report.

   Student A: Summarize the main ideas of the report.

   Student B: Tell your partner if you agree with his or her summary.

2. Listen to the interview.

   Student B: Summarize the main ideas of the interview.

   Student A: Tell your partner if you agree with his or her summary.

iQ PRACTICE Go online for more practice with summarizing.
Practice > Unit 7 > Activity 14

Role-play an interview

In this section, you are going to role-play an interview. As you prepare your role play, think about the Unit Question, "How do people survive in extreme environments?" Use information from Listening 1, Listening 2, and your work in this unit to prepare your role play. Refer to the Self-Assessment checklist on page 158.

CONSIDER THE IDEAS

🔊 **A. INVESTIGATE** Listen to the interview about an extreme environment. Number the interviewer's questions in the order you hear them, from 1 to 5.

____ How cold does it get in the winter?

____ Is it true that it's dark all the time in the winter?

____ What about food? What did you eat?

____ Have you ever lived in a really extreme environment?

____ How do you keep warm?

🔊 **B. INVESTIGATE** Listen again and take notes about Farouk's answers.

C. CREATE Work with a partner. Use the questions and your notes to act out the conversation. Answer the questions using your own words. Take turns being the interviewer.

PREPARE AND SPEAK

A. GATHER IDEAS Work with your partner. Prepare to role-play an interview.

1. Decide who will be the interviewer and who will be the person interviewed. Choose a topic for your interview. The topics below are just ideas to help you get started. You can use one of these or your own idea.

   - Living through a heat wave
   - Life in a very cold place
   - Life high in the mountains
   - Living in the desert
   - Living where it's very wet
   - Living on another planet

2. Make notes about all you know about your topic.

B. ORGANIZE IDEAS With your partner, plan the interview.

1. Make a list of questions for the interview.

2. Make notes for the answers to each one. (Don't write out the whole interview. Just make notes.)

3. Prepare a summary of the interview. The interviewer will end the interview with this summary.

C. SPEAK Practice your interview. Use intonation to express feelings during the interview. Present your interview to the class. Refer to the Self-Assessment checklist on page 158 before you begin.

iQ PRACTICE Go online for your alternate Unit Assignment.
Practice > Unit 7 > Activity 15

CHECK AND REFLECT

A. CHECK Think about the Unit Assignment as you complete the Self-Assessment checklist.

SELF-ASSESSMENT	Yes	No
I was able to speak easily about the topic.	☐	☐
My partner and the class understood me.	☐	☐
I used the future tense with *will*.	☐	☐
I used vocabulary from the unit.	☐	☐
I summarized the main ideas in the interview.	☐	☐
I used the correct word stress in compound nouns.	☐	☐

B. REFLECT Discuss these questions with a partner or group.

1. What is something new you learned in this unit?

2. Look back at the Unit Question—How do people survive in extreme environments? Is your answer different now than when you started this unit? If yes, how is it different? Why?

iQ PRACTICE Go to the online discussion board to discuss the questions. *Practice > Unit 7 > Activity 16*

TRACK YOUR SUCCESS

iQ PRACTICE Go online to check the words and phrases you have learned in this unit. *Practice ❯ Unit 7 ❯ Activity 17*

Check (✓) the skills and strategies you learned. If you need more work on a skill, refer to the page(s) in parentheses.

NOTE-TAKING ☐ I can prepare to take notes in class. (p. 140)

CRITICAL THINKING ☐ I can categorize information. (p. 144)

LISTENING ☐ I can recognize a speaker's attitude. (p. 145)

VOCABULARY ☐ I can recognize and use compound nouns. (p. 150)

GRAMMAR ☐ I can recognize and use *will* to talk about the future. (p. 152)

PRONUNCIATION ☐ I can use correct word stress in compound nouns. (p. 153)

SPEAKING ☐ I can summarize information. (p. 154)

OBJECTIVE ▶ ☐ I can gather information and ideas to role-play an interview about surviving in extreme environments.

8 Public Health

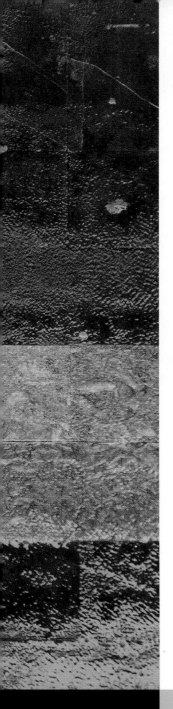

How important is cleanliness?

A. Discuss these questions with your classmates

1. Do you think you use a lot of water every day? Explain.

2. What did your parents tell you about cleanliness?

3. Look at the photo. What is the man doing? Do you think this is important?

B. Listen to *The Q Classroom* online. Then answer these questions.

1. How are Yuna's and Felix's answers to the question different?

2. What does Marcus say about the importance of clean water?

3. What does Sophy say about the other opinions?

iQ PRACTICE Go to the online discussion board to discuss the Unit Question with your classmates. *Practice > Unit 8 > Activity 1*

UNIT OBJECTIVE

Watch a video and listen to a follow-up discussion. Then listen to a lecture. Gather information and ideas to participate in a discussion about the importance of clean water.

LISTENING 1   Water for Life

OBJECTIVE ▶

You are going to watch a video and then listen to a follow-up discussion about the importance of clean water. As you watch and listen, gather information and ideas about the importance of cleanliness.

PREVIEW THE LISTENING

A. VOCABULARY Here are some words and phrases from Listening 1. Choose the answer that has the meaning closest to the <u>underlined</u> word or phrase.

1. There is a <u>shortage</u> of fruit this year. The winter was too cold and many of the fruit trees died.

    a. large amount   b. not enough   c. too much

2. As the number of people increases, the <u>demand</u> for water also increases.

    a. need   b. kind   c. place

3. The <u>climate</u> here is good for crops. It rains often and it's not too cold.

    a. weather   b. land   c. ocean

4. The town tried to <u>prevent</u> the state from building another road. They didn't succeed, and the new roadwork begins this month.

    a. let   b. stop   c. allow

5. The tomato plants in my garden had a <u>disease</u>. Many of the leaves turned brown, and some of the plants died.

    a. energy   b. sickness   c. health

6. <u>Agriculture</u> uses a lot of water. Both animals and plants need water to be healthy.

    a. farming   b. city life   c. space

ACADEMIC LANGUAGE
The verb *prevent* is often used in academic English. It is sometimes used with the preposition *from* and an *-ing* verb. *The doctors prevented the disease from spreading.*

⌐ **OPAL**
Oxford Phrasal Academic Lexicon

7. Because there is a <u>lack of</u> water, we have to try to use less every day.

   a. not enough   b. too much   c. a lot of

8. Building another dam will have serious <u>consequences</u>. For example, some people who live near the river above the dam will lose their homes.

   a. ideas   b. problems   c. results

9. We need to have a good <u>supply</u> of food and water, in case of a storm. We'll need enough for two weeks.

   a. quality   b. type   c. amount

10. If more businesses come to the city, the population will <u>grow</u>.

   a. become smaller   b. get larger   c. decline

iQ PRACTICE Go online for more practice with the vocabulary.
Practice ⟩ Unit 8 ⟩ Activities 2–3

TIP FOR SUCCESS
Many students are nervous about listening. Relax! If you are nervous or stressed, it's more difficult to listen and understand what you hear.

B. PREVIEW You are going to watch a video and then listen to a group discussion about the importance of clean water. What are two problems you think the video or the discussion will mention? Discuss with a partner.

WORK WITH THE LISTENING

iQ RESOURCES Go online to watch the video.
Resources ⟩ Video ⟩ Unit 8 ⟩ Listening Part 1

A. LISTEN AND TAKE NOTES Create an outline like the one below. Watch the video* and then listen to the discussion. As you watch and listen, add ideas to your outline. Try to add a few key words in each section.

VOCABULARY SKILL REVIEW
In Unit 7, you learned about compound nouns. What compound nouns can you identify in Listening 1 Part 1?

iQ RESOURCES Go online to download extra vocabulary support.
Resources ⟩ Extra Vocabulary ⟩ Unit 8

Part 1: Video	Part 2: Discussion
A. Uses for water	A. Children and water-related disease
B. Things that take a lot of water to make	B. Population growth in cities
C. Sources of clean water	C. Water quality

*Audio version available. *Resources ⟩ Audio ⟩ Unit 8*

B. EXPAND Watch the video and listen to the discussion again. Add more information to your notes.

C. IDENTIFY Read the questions. Choose the correct answers. Use your notes to help you. Then watch and listen to check your answers.

1. Compared to 100 years ago, how much more water do we use now?

   a. about sixty times as much

   b. about six times as much

   c. about sixteen times as much

2. What solution does the video suggest for the world's water problems?

   a. taking more water from rivers

   b. learning how to use ocean water

   c. reducing the demand for water

3. Where did Marie get the information about the numbers of people living in cities?

   a. a report by the United States government

   b. a report from the European Union

   c. a report issued by the United Nations

4. What does Marie say about the population around Lake Chad?

   a. It's decreasing.

   b. It's increasing.

   c. It isn't changing.

5. What do the students say they will do after the discussion?

    a. organize their ideas and information

    b. review all of their data

    c. watch the video again

 D. IDENTIFY Work with a partner. Complete the chart with numbers from the box. Use your notes to help you. Then watch and listen again to check your answers.

120	more than 55	over 300 million trillion	38 million
29.8	8,000	over one billion	

1. Gallons of water on Earth	
2. Number of people without clean drinking water	
3. Liters of water needed to produce one cup of coffee	
4. Liters of water needed to produce one hamburger	
5. Percent of world's population living in cities in 1950	
6. Percent of world's population living in cities in 2017	
7. Population living around Lake Chad	

E. DISCUSS Work in a group. Take turns asking and answering the questions.

1. One cup of coffee has about one cup of water. One hamburger has one small piece of meat. How can you explain the large amount of water used to produce these things?

2. In the video, the speaker says that water shortages could "lead to wars." Why might this happen?

3. What kinds of solutions do you think the students will suggest for the world's water problems?

iQ PRACTICE Go online for additional listening and comprehension.
Practice > Unit 8 > Activity 4

 ## SAY WHAT YOU THINK

DISCUSS Discuss the questions in a group.

1. Imagine that you don't have enough water for basic things like drinking, cooking, and cleaning. How would this affect you? What could you do about it?

2. Jing and Marie talk about the number of people who die from water-related illnesses like cholera. How can this be prevented?

A **fact** is something that is true. It can be information about an event, information about a person, or a statistic.

> About two million children under five die every year from water-related illnesses.

An **opinion** is a person's belief or attitude about something. Opinions often have key words like *I think*, *I feel*, or *I'd say*. Most opinions also make value judgments.

> **I think** the lack of clean water is the **most serious** problem in the world today.

Opinions are neither true nor untrue. Opinions can be supported with facts.

> **Opinion:** I think the lack of clean water is the most serious problem in the world today.
>
> **Supporting fact:** The lack of clean water causes the deaths of about two million children under five every year.

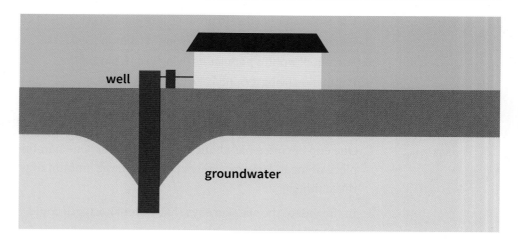

A. CATEGORIZE Listen to these comments from an online discussion about using underground water as a solution to the water problem. Write *fact* or *opinion* for each statement. Write down key words you hear that tell you that each statement is a fact or opinion.

Name	Fact or Opinion	Key Words
Paul	opinion	"seems to me"
Sara		
Liza		
Jamal		
Walaa		
Paul		

B. EVALUATE Work in a group. Compare your responses and notes in the chart in Activity A. If your responses are different, discuss and decide on the correct response. Then listen to the recording again with the group.

iQ PRACTICE Go online for more practice with recognizing facts and opinions. *Practice > Unit 8 > Activity 5*

NOTE-TAKING SKILL Using notes to write a summary

When you review your notes after a class, it can be helpful to write a short summary of the class discussion. Doing this will help you remember the main points. These are a few things to consider when writing a summary.

- Remember that a summary focuses only on the main ideas and does not include a lot of details.

- Notes use single words, short phrases, and many abbreviations. In the summary, you should use complete sentences and write words out fully.

- In a summary, you should try to use your own words to express ideas when possible.

A. EVALUATE Look at one student's notes about the video in Unit 7, *The Nomads of Outer Mongolia*. Then read the summary. Underline three (or more) examples of details that are NOT included in the summary.

A. Where
   Outer Mongolia
   Darhad Valley
   South of Siberia
B. Who?
   Darhad tribe — nomad
   no perm. settle.
C. Lifestyle
   animals / important food clothing
   dangers wolves, bad weather
   herd animals / good pastures
   live in two felt-lined tents "gers"
   gas stove, TV
D. Travel
   Mount. 3,000 m snow
   Wom. make food yogurt cheese
   return spring

The nomads of Outer Mongolia are called the Darhad people. Nomads move from one place to another during the year. Their animals are very important because they give them food and clothing. Bad weather and wolves are dangers they experience. In the winter, they travel over high mountains in the snow. They carry their tents and food with them. They need to find good pastures for their animals. They come back in the spring.

B. SYNTHESIZE Review your notes about the video and class discussion in Listening 1. Write a short summary of the main ideas that the students will include in their report about the importance of clean water.

C. EXTEND Work with a partner. Compare your summaries. Did you mention all the main ideas? Did you include any unnecessary details?

iQ PRACTICE Go online for more practice with using notes to write a summary. *Practice > Unit 8 > Activity 6*

Is It Possible to Be Too Clean?

OBJECTIVE ▶

You are going to listen to a lecture about the connection between cleanliness and the immune system. The immune system in the human body protects us from disease. As you listen, gather information and ideas about the importance of cleanliness.

PREVIEW THE LISTENING

A. VOCABULARY Here are some words from Listening 2. Read the definitions. Then complete each sentence with the correct word.

---

allergy (*noun*) a condition that makes you sick when you eat or touch something that does not normally make people sick

automatically (*adverb*) done by itself; without human control

bacteria (*noun*) 🍗 very tiny living things

defense (*noun*) 🍗 protection of something from an attack

digest (*verb*) to change food in the stomach so it can be used by the body

dirt (*noun*) 🍗 a thing that isn't clean, like dust or mud

germs (*noun*) tiny living things that cause disease

old-fashioned (*adjective*) not modern

sensible (*adjective*) 🍗 having good judgment; being reasonable

---

🍗 Oxford 3000™ words   **OPAL** Oxford Phrasal Academic Lexicon

1. Did you know that yogurt is made with two kinds of "good" _____? They turn milk into yogurt. There are thousands in every cup.

2. Let's see, Ashley can't eat chocolate or strawberries. She can't have any pets in the house. And don't ever give her flowers. She has a terrible _____ problem.

3. You don't have to turn off my computer. It will turn off _____ in two hours.

4. Yogurt may not upset your stomach like other milk products. In fact, it helps you _____ your food.

5. I have a special program on my computer as a _____ against viruses that may attack it.

6. Please take your muddy shoes off before you come in the house. I don't want _____ all over my clean floor.

7. Michael decided not to go out tonight because he has an important test tomorrow. That was a(n) _____ decision.

8. I've had this dress for 20 years. It looks extremely _____ now.

9. Please cover your mouth when you cough. You're spreading your _____ all over. I don't want to get sick.

iQ PRACTICE Go online for more practice with the vocabulary.
Practice > Unit 8 > Activities 7–8

B. PREVIEW You are going to listen to a lecture about the connection between cleanliness and the immune system. Work with a partner. Discuss these questions: Is it possible to be too clean? Why or why not?

WORK WITH THE LISTENING

A. LISTEN AND TAKE NOTES Listen to the lecture and take notes. Use the outline to help you.

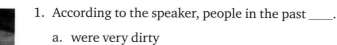

Is it poss. to be too clean?
A   Change in attitudes re: dirt
  - Past
  - Present

B   Studies re: germs
  - Germany
  - Australia
C   Conclusion

B. SYNTHESIZE Use your notes to write a short summary of the lecture. Then compare your notes and summary with a partner.

C. ANALYZE Read the sentences. Choose the answer that best completes each statement. Then listen and check your answers.

1. According to the speaker, people in the past ____.

   a. were very dirty

   b. were much more worried about cleanliness than we are today

   c. were more relaxed about touching dirt

2. One study showed that children living in an environment with fewer germs ____.

   a. developed fewer allergies

   b. didn't develop strong immune systems

   c. never got sick

3. The speaker says that ____.

   a. some bacteria are good for us

   b. all bacteria cause disease

   c. bacteria are not necessary

D. CATEGORIZE Read the statements. Write *T* (true) or *F* (false). Then correct the false statements.

____ 1. The speaker's grandmother might let her eat cookies that fell on the floor.

____ 2. Carrying hand sanitizer in your pocket is an old-fashioned custom.

____ 3. We should stop taking regular baths and let our houses get dirty.

____ 4. The German study showed that children who lived in cities and had no pets were healthier than kids who lived on farms.

____ 5. In Australia, some people are giving kids "dirt pills" because they think this will help them develop a defense against asthma.

____ 6. Bacteria are necessary in order to create compost from food waste.

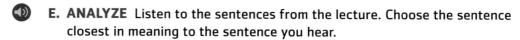

E. ANALYZE Listen to the sentences from the lecture. Choose the sentence closest in meaning to the sentence you hear.

1. a. Dirt, germs, and bacteria are harmful to our immune systems.

   b. People nowadays spend too much time cleaning and bathing.

   c. A little contact with dirt and germs helps build our defense against disease.

2. a. Some Australian children with asthma are taking "dirt" pills. The pills have bacteria the children did not come into contact with as babies.

   b. In Australia, more children are getting asthma because they touched the bacteria that cause the disease when they were babies.

   c. In Australia, little babies are taking "dirt pills" so they won't get asthma.

3. a. People should all be a lot dirtier.

   b. Some people today are a little bit too clean.

   c. Some people today are too dirty.

F. EXPLAIN Do hand sanitizers work? Work in a group. Read the explanation and study the charts. Then answer the questions.

A group of doctors did a study in an elementary school. They gave hand sanitizers to the students in some classrooms (Group A), but not in others (Group B). Then they counted the number of days students were absent because of illness, either stomach illnesses or colds. The study continued for eight weeks.

Absences for stomach illnesses

	0	1	2	3	Total days absent
Group A	123	15	6	2	33
Group B	105	21	9	3	48

Absences for colds

	0	1	2	3	Total days absent
Group A	106	22	10	3	51
Group B	104	19	10	5	54

1. Which group had more days absent because of stomach illnesses?

2. Which group had more days absent because of colds?

3. How are the results for stomach illnesses and colds different?

4. Do you think that this study proves that hand sanitizers help keep children healthier?

SAY WHAT YOU THINK

SYNTHESIZE Think about Listening 1 and Listening 2 as you discuss the questions.

1. Before Listening 2, you discussed the question "Is it possible to be too clean?" How did you answer this question before listening? What is your answer now? Did it change? Why or why not?

2. Do you worry about contact with germs? Why or why not?

3. As countries around the world become more modern, the demand for water will grow. What can people do about this?

4. Imagine that someone advised you to "let your children play in the dirt." How would you reply?

VOCABULARY SKILL Using the dictionary

Dictionaries have many different kinds of information about words. In addition to the meaning of the word, a dictionary entry includes:

- part of speech—for example, *noun*, *verb*, *adjective*
- word forms, such as plurals, past tense, and participle forms, and comparatives
- pronunciation
- grammatical information about words—for example, countability of nouns [C for *countable*, U for *uncountable*]

An entry can also include:

- some synonyms or antonyms (opposites)
- example phrases and sentences

TIP FOR SUCCESS

When possible, use an English learner's dictionary. It gives simple definitions and examples of words.

A. IDENTIFY Read the dictionary entry for the word *disease*. Then mark the different kinds of information.

1. Circle the pronunciation information.

2. Underline the part of speech.

3. Put a check (✓) above the grammar information.

4. Put a star (★) next to the example sentences or phrases.

> **dis·ease** /dɪˈziz/ *noun* [C, U] (**HEALTH**) an illness of the body in humans, animals, or plants: *an infectious disease* ◆ *Rats and flies spread disease.* ▶ **diseased** *adj.*: *His diseased kidney had to be removed.*

All dictionary entries adapted from the *Oxford American Dictionary for learners of English* © Oxford University Press 2011.

B. INVESTIGATE Use a dictionary to answer the questions about the bold words. Sometimes you may need to look at words before or after the bold word to find the answer.

1. Is the word **bacteria** singular or plural? _____

2. What's an adjective in the same word family as the noun **sanitation**?

   _____

3. What's the verb in the same word family as the noun **defense**?

   _____

4. What's the adverb form of the adjective **sensible**? _____

5. In Listening 2, the speaker says, "No one is saying that we should stop **bathing**." How do you spell the base form of the verb **bathing**?

   _____

6. Do you pronounce the *th* in **asthma**? _____

C. ANALYZE Read the sentences. Identify the error in each sentence. Then rewrite each sentence to correct the error.

1. Some bacteria doesn't make you sick.

   <u>Some bacteria don't make you sick.</u>

2. The kitchen in that restaurant is not sanitation.

   _____

3. Don't worry about me! I can defense myself if there's a problem.

   _____

4. After that big storm, I think it's very sensibly to start boiling our drinking water.

   _____

5. My sister baths her baby before bed. The warm water relaxes him.

   _____

6. We can't have a cat because my son has asma.

   _____

iQ PRACTICE Go online for more practice using the dictionary.
Practice > Unit 8 > Activity 9

SPEAKING

OBJECTIVE ▶

At the end of this unit, you are going to participate in a group discussion about a problem related to water and sanitation. You will present a solution to the problem and try to persuade others that your solution is the best one.

GRAMMAR *If* clauses for future possibility

If clauses can express future possibility. Sentences with *if* clauses show a cause-and-effect relationship. The *if* clause describes the cause. The result clause gives a possible effect.

The verb in the *if* clause is in the simple present. The result clause uses a modal, such as **will**, **can**, or **may/might** + **verb**. The choice depends on how certain the speaker is about the result.

if clause	result clause
If there **is** a lack of clean water,	diseases **will spread** very quickly.
If you **use** hand sanitizer,	you **might not get** sick this winter.

Note: The *if* clause and the result clause can come in either order. When the *if* clause is first, it is followed by a comma. There's no comma when the result clause is first.

☐ Diseases will spread very quickly if there is a lack of clean water.

iQ RESOURCES   Go online to watch the Grammar Skill Video.
Resources > Video > Unit 8 > Grammar Skill Video

 A. CATEGORIZE Listen to the sentences. Write the cause and the effect in each sentence.

	Cause	Effect
1	test the water	find out it's polluted
2		
3		
4		
5		

B. COMPOSE Look at the words and phrases below. Use the words and phrases to write sentences with *if* clauses.

1. they / use the underground water source / have water for 400 years

   _____

   _____

2. I / use hand sanitizer / might not get sick

   _____

3. we / not get rain / crops / die

   _____

4. Sarah / save more water / take shorter showers

   _____

5. people / have clean water / be fewer deaths

   _____

6. John / spread germs / not wash his hands

   _____

C. EVALUATE Compare your sentences with a partner. Take turns saying your sentences.

iQ PRACTICE Go online for more practice with *if* clauses for future possibility. *Practice > Unit 8 > Activity 10*

iQ PRACTICE Go online for the Grammar Expansion: future time clauses. *Practice > Unit 8 > Activity 11*

PRONUNCIATION Function words and stress

Function words are the short words that connect the content words in a sentence. Function words are usually not stressed. They are also pronounced more quickly than content words. They can include words like these.

articles: *the, a, an*

pronouns: *he, she, it*

prepositions: *in, on, at, for*

forms of the verbs *be, do,* or *have*

conjunctions: *and, but, or*

modals such as *can* or *will*

The bold words in this sentence are function words.

People use special soaps **that** kill germs, **and** they carry hand sanitizers **in their** pockets.

A. IDENTIFY Read the paragraph. Underline the function words. Then listen and focus on the pronunciation of the function words.

There is no new water on Earth. All of the water on Earth—the rivers, lakes, oceans, ice at the North and South Poles, clouds, and rain—is about one billion years old. The water moves around the planet. It can change to ice, to rain, or to fog, but it's always the same water. Think about it. The population of the world is growing, but the supply of water is always the same.

B. APPLY Work with a partner. Take turns reading the paragraph in Activity A. Make sure you stress the content words and not the function words.

C. APPLY Some of the function words in this paragraph are missing. Listen and write the missing function words.

"Water, water, everywhere, nor any drop to drink." Those

_____are_____ the words _____ the famous English
　　 1 　　　　　　　　　　　　　 2

poet Samuel Coleridge. He was writing about _____ man
　　　　　　　　　　　　　　　　　　　　　　　　　　　　　　 3

alone _____ a boat on _____ ocean. The words
　　　　　　 4 　　　　　　　　　　　　　 5

might also describe _____ condition _____
　　　　　　　　　　　　　 6 　　　　　　　　　　 7

the people _____ our planet. Earth has about 1.4 billion cubic
　　　　　　　 8

kilometers _____ water. The problem _____
                          9   10
that 97.5 percent _____ that water is salt water in the
                                    11
oceans _____ the seas. Only 2.5 percent is fresh water. Most
                  12
_____ that fresh water _____ in the ice at the
            13   14
North _____ South Poles or underground. Only 0.3 percent of
              15
_____ fresh water is in lakes _____ rivers where
            16   17
people _____ easily find and use _____.
                  18   19

D. APPLY Practice reading the paragraph in Activity C with a partner.

iQ PRACTICE   Go online for more practice with function words and stress.
Practice > Unit 8 > Activity 12

 CRITICAL THINKING STRATEGY

Appraising solutions to problems

When you listen to other people suggest solutions to a problem, you need to **appraise** what they are saying. To appraise means to analyze, assess, and make a judgment about their solutions. You might then decide whether you agree or disagree. You might also decide that you need more information.

iQ PRACTICE   Go online to watch the Critical Thinking Video and check your comprehension. *Practice > Unit 8 > Activity 13*

E. INVESTIGATE Read the case study below. What problem does it describe? Discuss with a partner.

There is a beautiful, clean river that comes down from the mountains. There are several villages on the banks of the river, and the people use the water for washing, cooking, and drinking. The problem is that some of the farmers in this area bring their animals down to the river to drink. This means that the animal waste gets into the water and pollutes it. The water is no longer safe. People who live near the river want the farmers to stop using the river for the animals.

F. EVALUATE Read the solutions some people have suggested. Appraise each statement. Mark each as *A* (agree), *D* (disagree) or *N* (need more information), depending on what you decide for each.

_____ 1. Residents should build fences along the river to prevent animals from getting to the water.

_____ 2. Residents should meet with the farmers to discuss the problem.

_____ 3. Residents should look for other ways to bring water to the animals. For example, they could build a system that brings water from the river to where the animals are.

_____ 4. Residents should ask the government to dig a community well, away from the river. This water would be for people, so they don't need to use the river water. Then the farmers could continue to take their animals to the river.

_____ 5. Residents should have the water tested, so they know exactly what the problems are with the water quality.

G. EXPLAIN Work with a group. Compare and discuss your answers. Give reasons to support your opinions. If you need more information for some solutions, what questions would you ask?

Participating in a group discussion can be challenging for a language learner. Here are a few suggestions to help you.

- Listen carefully to what others are saying. Listen for the topic of the discussion and the main ideas.

- When you speak, start by referring to something the previous speaker said. Make sure your comment relates to the topic.

- Speak clearly and be sure to speak loudly enough for people to hear you.

- Don't interrupt people. Wait for a break in the conversation before you speak.

- Help others participate by asking questions and saying things like, "Mary, we haven't heard your ideas yet."

A. DISCUSS Listen to parts of the conversation in Listening 1. Discuss the questions with a partner.

Part 1

1. How does Jing invite Marie to participate in the conversation?

2. How do you know that Marie was listening to what Jing said?

Part 2

3. What's the problem with Toby's comment about being too clean?

4. What does Emma say to Toby? How does this help the conversation?

Part 3

5. How does Marie speak at the start—very softly or firmly and clearly? Is this a problem? Why or why not?

6. What does Jing do to Marie?

7. What does Emma do about it?

8. What does Jing say at the end?

B. CREATE Work in a group. Choose one of the following topics or use your own idea. Talk about it for five minutes. During that time, everyone in the group should speak at least once. Use the suggestions in the Speaking Skill box.

Three things we can do now to save water

Two things we can do to make our city cleaner

What we should teach children about cleanliness

iQ PRACTICE Go online for more practice with participating in a group discussion. *Practice > Unit 8 > Activity 14*

Give a persuasive presentation

In this section, you are going to give a persuasive presentation. As you prepare your presentation, think about the Unit Question, "How important is cleanliness?" Use information from Listening 1, Listening 2, and your work in this unit to support your presentation. Refer to the Self-Assessment checklist on page 182.

CONSIDER THE IDEAS

INVESTIGATE With a partner, read the case studies about issues related to water and sanitation. For each case, discuss the questions.

1. What problem does the case present?

2. Who are the people involved?

3. How do the people agree or disagree about the situation?

Case 1

A city has a serious problem with its water supply. For several years there has been very little rain. The lake that supplies the city with water is getting smaller and smaller. The city officials are telling people that they have to use less water. But most people don't seem to understand this. They don't want to change the way they use water. One official says, "If people won't change, we will soon have to start rationing water. That means that we would give people only a small amount of water each day. No one will like that!"

Case 2

The principal and a group of teachers at a high school want to provide hand sanitizer in the classrooms. They think that if teachers and students use these frequently, fewer people will get sick from colds and flu. Many parents and some teachers are against this idea. They say that this is taking cleanliness too far. They say hand sanitizers are not a substitute for soap and water. They say the best way to keep your hands clean is to wash them for at least 15 seconds with warm water and soap. They point out that the bathrooms at the school are often out of soap. They're telling the principal, "Buy more soap, not hand sanitizer!"

PREPARE AND SPEAK

TIP FOR SUCCESS

As you participate in these activities, try to follow the suggestions for participating in group discussions.

A. GATHER IDEAS Work in a group. Choose one of the cases in the Consider the Ideas section. Then follow these steps. Use the chart to help you organize your ideas.

1. Review the case and make sure everyone understands the problem.

2. Brainstorm possible solutions for the problem.

3. For each solution, think of any pros (advantages) or cons (disadvantages) there might be. What will the people involved think of the solution? Will they accept it?

Case Study: _____

Solutions	Pros and Cons
1.	Pro:
	Con:
2.	Pro:
	Con:
3.	Pro:
	Con:

B. ORGANIZE IDEAS As a group, prepare a presentation of the case you picked and the best solutions. Each person in the group should be responsible for one possible solution. During the presentation, you will try to persuade your audience that your solution is best.

C. SPEAK Present your case and the solutions to the class. After the presentation, discuss these questions with the class. Refer to the Self-Assessment checklist below before you begin.

1. Ask the class, "Did you agree or disagree with our solutions? Why or why not?"

2. What other solutions can you think of for this case?

iQ PRACTICE Go online for your alternate Unit Assignment.
Practice > Unit 8 > Activity 15

CHECK AND REFLECT

A. CHECK Think about the Unit Assignment as you complete the Self-Assessment checklist.

SELF-ASSESSMENT	Yes	No
I was able to speak easily about the topic.	☐	☐
My partner, group, and class understood me.	☐	☐
I used *if* clauses for future possibility.	☐	☐
I used vocabulary from the unit.	☐	☐
I participated in a group discussion.	☐	☐
I used correct stress for function words.	☐	☐

B. REFLECT Discuss these questions with a partner or group.

1. What is something new you learned in this unit?

2. Look back at the Unit Question—How important is cleanliness? Is your answer different now than when you started this unit? If yes, how is it different? Why?

iQ PRACTICE Go to the online discussion board to discuss the questions.
Practice > Unit 8 > Activity 16

TRACK YOUR SUCCESS

iQ PRACTICE Go online to check the words and phrases you have learned in this unit. *Practice > Unit 8 > Activity 17*

Check (✓) the skills and strategies you learned. If you need more work on a skill, refer to the page(s) in parentheses.

LISTENING	☐ I can recognize facts and opinions. (p. 166)
NOTE-TAKING	☐ I can use notes to write a summary. (p. 167)
VOCABULARY	☐ I can use the dictionary to find information about words. (p. 172)
GRAMMAR	☐ I can use *if* clauses for future possibility. (p. 174)
PRONUNCIATION	☐ I can stress function words properly. (p. 175)
CRITICAL THINKING	☐ I can appraise solutions to a problem. (p. 177)
SPEAKING	☐ I can participate in a group discussion. (p. 179)

OBJECTIVE ▶ ☐ I can gather information and ideas to participate in a discussion about the importance of clean water.

The Oxford 3000™ is a list of the 3,000 core words that every learner of English needs to know. The words have been chosen based on their frequency in the Oxford English Corpus and relevance to learners of English. Every word is aligned to the CEFR, guiding learners on the words they should know at the A1–B2 level.

OPAL The Oxford Phrasal Academic Lexicon is an essential guide to the most important words and phrases to know for academic English. The word lists are based on the Oxford Corpus of Academic English and the British Academic Spoken English corpus.

The Common European Framework of Reference for Language (CEFR) provides a basic description of what language learners have to do to use language effectively. The system contains 6 reference levels: A1, A2, B1, B2, C1, C2.

verb + adj

UNIT 1

advertise (v.) A2
affordable (adj.) B2
brake (n.)
buck the trend (v. phr.)
chat (v.) A2
decline (v.) OPAL B2
enormous (adj.) A2
essential (adj.) OPAL B1
failure (n.) OPAL B2
get the point (v. phr.)
postage (n.)
potential (adj.) OPAL B2
realize (v.) A2
reasonable (adj.) OPAL B2
wealthy (adj.) B2
wheel (n.) A2

UNIT 2

beautiful (adj.) A1
blend in (v. phr.)
brilliant (adj.) A2
hide (v.) A2
insect (n.) A2
match (v.) B1
peaceful (adj.) B1

poison (n.) B1
predator (n.) C1
pride (n.) B2
shape (n.) OPAL A2
skin (n.) A2
solid (adj.) B1
straight (adj.) A2
survive (v.) B1
warning (n.) B1
wing (n.) B1

violent (adj.)
The Man is a very violent person

UNIT 3

admit (v.) B1
attentive (adj.)
behavior (n.) OPAL A2
be courteous (adj.) *I'm courteous*
have courtesy (n.) C1 *I have courtesy*
deal with (v. phr.) A2 *= cope with*
etiquette (n.)
improve (v.) OPAL A1
increase (n.) OPAL A2 ✓
influence (n.) OPAL B1
manners (n.) A2
polite (adj.) A2
principal (n.) B2
respect (n.) OPAL B1

rude (adj.) A2
scream (v.) B2
shout out (v. phr.)
society (n.) OPAL A2 *economic 社會*
valuable (adj.) OPAL B1
violence (n.) OPAL B2
Violence has been increasing since the pandemic

UNIT 4

common (adj.) OPAL A1
dependent on (adj. phr.) OPAL B2
digital (adj.) OPAL A2
disconnect (v.)
face-to-face (adj. phr. / adv. phr.)
find (v.) OPAL B1
forever (adv.) B2
friendship (n.) B1
headline (n.) B1
meaningful (adj.) OPAL C1
post (v.) A1
privacy (n.) B2
relationship (n.) OPAL A2
scary (adj.) A2
silly (adj.) B1
strange (adj.) A2

This school has strict rules about courtesy.

I'm very courteous in school
It's important to be courteous in social situation.

184

UNIT 5

ancestor *(n.)* B2
appearance *(n.)* A2
coincidence *(n.)* B2
cousin *(n.)* A1
database *(n.)* B2
get along *(v. phr.)*
identity *(n.)* OPAL B1
inherit *(v.)* B2
input *(n.)* OPAL B2
participant *(n.)* OPAL B2
record *(n.)* OPAL A2
search *(v.)* A2
separate *(adj.)* OPAL A2
slave *(n.)* B2
tendency *(n.)* OPAL B2
twin *(n.)* A2

UNIT 6

apply *(v.)* OPAL B2
benefit *(n.)* OPAL A2
coach *(n.)* A2
competitive *(adj.)* B1
developer *(n.)*
disappointment *(n.)* B2
entertainment *(n.)* B1
lose *(v.)* A1

object *(n.)* OPAL B2
positive *(adj.)* OPAL A1
pressure *(n.)* OPAL B1
react *(v.)* OPAL A2
stress *(n.)* OPAL A2
tournament *(n.)* B2
useful *(adj.)* OPAL A1
wonderful *(adj.)* A1

UNIT 7

attack *(v.)* OPAL A2
earthquake *(n.)* B1
elevator *(n.)*
fascinating *(adj.)* B1
freezing *(adj.)*
height *(n.)* A2
neighborhood *(n.)* B1
permanent *(adj.)* B2
process *(v.)* OPAL B2
remain *(v.)* B1
resident *(n.)* OPAL B2
response *(n.)* OPAL A2
shake *(v.)* A2
suburb *(n.)* B2
suitable *(adj.)* OPAL B1
threat *(n.)* OPAL B2

UNIT 8

agriculture *(n.)* B2
allergy *(n.)*
automatically *(adv.)* B2
bacteria *(n.)* B2
climate *(n.)* OPAL A2
consequence *(n.)* OPAL B1
defense *(n.)* B2
demand *(n.)* OPAL B2
digest *(v.)*
dirt *(n.)* B1
disease *(n.)* A2
germs *(n.)*
grow *(v.)* OPAL A1
lack of *(n. phr.)*
old-fashioned *(adj.)* B1
prevent *(v.)* OPAL A2
sensible *(adj.)* B1
shortage *(n.)* B2
supply *(n.)* OPAL B1

(I break it) (I broke it) (It's broken)

break   broke   broken

AUTHOR

Margaret Brooks worked for many years as a teacher and administrator in a variety of English language-teaching programs in the Dominican Republic and Costa Rica, including serving as a professor at the Autonomous University of Santo Domingo and working with a private company to develop specialized language courses for businesses in Costa Rica. She has also written and developed course material for a wide range of ELT programs.

SERIES CONSULTANTS

Lawrence J. Zwier holds an M.A. in TESL from the University of Minnesota. He is currently the Associate Director for Curriculum Development at the English Language Center at Michigan State University in East Lansing. He has taught ESL/EFL in the United States, Saudi Arabia, Malaysia, Japan, and Singapore.

Marguerite Ann Snow holds a Ph.D. in Applied Linguistics from UCLA. She teaches in the TESOL M.A. program in the Charter College of Education at California State University, Los Angeles. She was a Fulbright scholar in Hong Kong and Cyprus. In 2006, she received the President's Distinguished Professor award at CSULA. She has trained ESL teachers in the United States and EFL teachers in more than 25 countries. She is the author/editor of numerous publications in the areas of content-based instruction, English for academic purposes, and standards for English teaching and learning. She is a co-editor of *Teaching English as a Second or Foreign Language* (4th ed.).

CRITICAL THINKING CONSULTANT **James Dunn** is a Junior Associate Professor at Tokai University and the Coordinator of the JALT Critical Thinking Special Interest Group. His research interests include critical thinking skills' impact on student brain function during English learning as measured by EEG. His educational goals are to help students understand that they are capable of more than they might think and to expand their cultural competence with critical thinking and higher-order thinking skills.

ASSESSMENT CONSULTANT **Elaine Boyd** has worked in assessment for over 30 years for international testing organizations. She has designed and delivered courses in assessment literacy and is also the author of several EL exam coursebooks for leading publishers. She is an Associate Tutor (M.A. TESOL/Linguistics) at University College, London. Her research interests are classroom assessment, issues in managing feedback, and intercultural competences.

VOCABULARY CONSULTANT **Cheryl Boyd Zimmerman** is Professor Emeritus at California State University, Fullerton. She specialized in second-language vocabulary acquisition, an area in which she is widely published. She taught graduate courses on second-language acquisition, culture, vocabulary, and the fundamentals of TESOL, and has been a frequent invited speaker on topics related to vocabulary teaching and learning. She is the author of *Word Knowledge: A Vocabulary Teacher's Handbook* and Series Director of *Inside Reading, Inside Writing,* and *Inside Listening and Speaking,* published by Oxford University Press.

ONLINE INTEGRATION **Chantal Hemmi** holds an Ed.D. TEFL and is a Japan-based teacher trainer and curriculum designer. Since leaving her position as Academic Director of the British Council in Tokyo, she has been teaching at the Center for Language Education and Research at Sophia University in an EAP/CLIL program offered for undergraduates. She delivers lectures and teacher trainings throughout Japan, Indonesia, and Malaysia.

COMMUNICATIVE GRAMMAR CONSULTANT **Nancy Schoenfeld** holds an M.A. in TESOL from Biola University in La Mirada, California, and has been an English language instructor since 2000. She has taught ESL in California and Hawaii and EFL in Thailand and Kuwait. She has also trained teachers in the United States and Indonesia. Her interests include teaching vocabulary, extensive reading, and student motivation. She is currently an English Language Instructor at Kuwait University.